DIETRICH MATESCHITZ:
WINGS FOR PEOPLE AND IDEAS

VOLKER VIECHTBAUER

DIETRICH MATESCHITZ: WINGS FOR PEOPLE AND IDEAS

Red Bull and Viktor Frankl's search for meaning

The penguin story (p. 130/131) was re-narrated and cited by courtesy of Dr. Eckart von Hirschhausen from: *Glück kommt selten allein*, Rowohlt Verlag, Reinbeck bei Hamburg 2009.

Despite making every effort to be accurate and researching carefully, the authors respectively editor and the publisher take no responsibility and accept no liability for the content provided.

1st Printing
© 2023 Benevento Verlag by Benevento Publishing Salzburg – Munich, a brand of Red Bull Media House GmbH, Wals near Salzburg

All rights reserved, in whole or in part, especially the right of public lecture/ recitation, the right to transmit by radio and television, and the translation right. No part of this publication may be reproduced in any form or by any means – graphic, electronic or mechanical (which includes but is not limited to: photocopying, recording, taping or storing information) – without the written permission of Red Bull Media House GmbH.

Publisher and Owner: Red Bull Media House GmbH
Oberst-Lepperdinger-Straße 11–15
5071 Wals near Salzburg, Austria

Layout and Typesetting: MEDIA DESIGN: RIZNER.AT
Typeset in Palatino, Futura PT
Cover design: Büro Jorge Schmidt, München
Copyright cover motive: © Hoika Mikhail / shutterstock
Printed by CPI Books in Germany
ISBN: 978-3-96704-129-3

*For my Uncle Herbert,
who sought freedom with us on so many journeys*

"Strictly speaking, the so-called 'World of Red Bull' no longer has much to do with the classic term 'Consumer Marketing', but is rather a sort of philosophy or worldview. This includes a certain amount of commitment to achieve, a judicious measure of risk, and the joy of bringing something to a successful conclusion as well as the necessary balance with sport, pleasure, music, entertainment, and social acceptance.
Red Bull has a number of success factors to choose from. Consistency, motivation, expertise, and common sense are among them. Or taking pleasure in what you do. Gratitude for success. And perhaps most importantly of all: a positive basic approach to life, work, and achievement.
And in addition, I agree with Viktor Frankl, who describes the right to personal responsibility as the most characteristic of all human rights."

Dietrich Mateschitz

CONTENTS

Preface   9

Introduction   13

I THE VALUES SYSTEM OF VIKTOR FRANKL AND THE CORPORATE CULTURE OF RED BULL

1 Freedom and personal responsibility   25
 How the foundation for a modern concern was laid in the early years of Red Bull   29

2 The will to find meaning, or the nature of tasks in life   37
 How Red Bull created a new market without taking itself too seriously ...   46
 ... And finally conquered the world from its base in Austria   54

3 Esteem, confidence, and trust   65
 How Red Bull set the parameters for a wealth of ideas and creativity   70

4 Paradoxical intention   85
 How Red Bull sounds out boundaries and surpasses itself   89

II HOW TO GIVE COMPANIES WINGS

   1 Viktor Frankl as the pioneer of a practiced humanism   117

     From talent to strength to purpose – a personal treasure hunt   127

   2 Martin Seligman, Don Clifton, and the invention of the strength test   151

     How the concern and employees at Red Bull achieve a meaningful approach to working together   162

Thoughts on the Future of Work – An Epilogue   193

Acknowledgments   211

Further Reading by Viktor Frankl   213

PREFACE

In the spring of 2020, after several months' work, I presented the first draft of this book to Dietrich Mateschitz to review and approve. I think he had certain reservations about the project from the very beginning: Why should we be publishing this book? What was the purpose of it all? he asked me when we touched briefly on the subject during our conversations.

My answer was that I wanted to use the book to explain the philosophy of Red Bull; that I wanted to provide new employees with a sort of orientation guide. But that I was sure that there was also a wider public that would be interested. So he asked me whether the book would also be available in bookstores. I responded that *he* should take that decision. "But it's already written, just publish it," he said. I insisted that he should read it and give it his approval.

The next reaction came several weeks later. He had started reading the manuscript and it seemed to me that he was satisfied. The manuscript was good, he commented, but a few mistakes had crept in which would need to be corrected. For example, the remark, "Not bad for a beverage company," in connection with four Formula One World Championship titles, came not from Bernie Ecclestone, but from Lewis Hamilton.* He was not referring to such inaccuracies, how-

---
* Of course this error has since been corrected.

ever. He thought we would have to meet up once or twice a week for several weeks and go through the whole thing.

More weeks passed before I inquired whether he had formed an opinion about the book yet. Dietrich Mateschitz said he had been pushing the subject to the back of his mind, but that he would tackle it now. Two or three weeks later he requested that I meet him in Thalgauegg, at the corporate headquarters of his private companies, a few kilometers from the concern headquarters in Fuschl am See. The news he had for me was not good. The book could not be published. The general tenor of his message was that Red Bull could not be attributed to one single formula or source—in this case Viktor Frankl. The concern was more multi-faceted than that. If I were to ask his long-standing assistant Sonja Ernstbrunner or CFO Walter Bachinger, they would all have a different view of Red Bull.

There it was again—the subjective perception of Red Bull, which he did not want to deprive any of the employees or consumers of (I shall refer to this in the book). Red Bull should remain a projection surface for the wishes and ambitions of those who had a connection to it.

At the end of our conversation he picked up the manuscript, which he had read in its entirety and had partly corrected (including the Ecclestone faux pas), and gave it to me with the comment: "But don't throw it away. Put it in the safe. Perhaps it could be a sort of obituary." And that was the end of the subject for the time being.

I am adding this preface on January 1, 2021, because I had a dream last night. Dietrich Mateschitz and I were sitting with some other people—perhaps employees—at a table, and were discussing a problem. It was evidently also about a contract. I had examined it from a legal point of view with regard to risks and—especially—ways of terminating it and what the consequences would be. What he demanded of me, of all of us sitting at that table, was to think about what was less obvious—about synergies, possibilities, and connections. Because "the sum of all the parts is greater than the whole."

Postscript: Shortly afterwards, Dietrich Mateschitz became seriously ill. He did not speak of his illness and continued to work. It was only shortly before his death that he gave us his instructions and wishes. On Saturday, October 22, 2022, his assistant Tina Deutner called me in the evening and asked me to send a message to the employees announcing the death of Dietrich Mateschitz. He had written it himself.

INTRODUCTION

// Life isn't about finding yourself. Life is about creating yourself. //

GEORGE BERNARD SHAW

Dietrich Mateschitz founded Red Bull at the end of the 1980s and launched the energy drink of the same name in Austria as the first functional drink outside Asia. The innovative marketing concept of Red Bull is taught today at business schools in Europe and beyond. Energy drinks are top in the global drinks ranking, beside Coca-Cola and Pepsi, and still have double-figure growth rates after more than thirty years, while traditional soft drinks are stagnating.

However, Red Bull is not just a drink; it is also an attitude to life. The brand stands for success, dynamism, innovation, independence, non-conformism, fun, and unpredictability. In contrast to the brand, the Red Bull of Dietrich Mateschitz is characterized by humanist qualities and is managed in line with conservative values. Its activities are determined by professionalism and modesty. And what may not be evident at first sight is that this conduct is based on the principles of Viktor Frankl.

Frankl was the founder of the third and last Viennese School of Psychotherapy, Logotherapy, and Existential Analysis, after Sigmund Freud and Alfred Adler. Frankl was a humanist. People and their specific task in life, their purpose, lay at the heart of his reflections. Individuals must choose this purpose for themselves freely and with personal responsibility, must stand up for it, pursue it unwaveringly, if necessary also against opposition, and with confidence in the possibility of a change in circumstances for the better.

At first glance, logotherapy has little in common with Red Bull. Their ways of thinking seem just too opposed—a search for meaning and existential analysis on the one hand, and fun and lifestyle on the other. And yet both are "phenomena" based on the same principles, which extend beyond their primary intention. They are a worldview, a worldview in fact which focuses above all on freedom, personal responsibility, and an absolute creative will.

Mateschitz attended Frankl's lectures personally. Frankl's practical humanism and the search for meaning struck a chord with the way of life of the founder, shareholder, and managing director Dietrich Mateschitz. They represent a practical alternative model to the permanent temptation to deny the (personal) responsibility of the individual.

Like Dietrich Mateschitz and Red Bull, Viktor Frankl also set out from Austria and conquered the world with his philosophy. Although both individuals lived according to comparable principles, Frankl was primarily a psychotherapist and a dogmatist, while Mateschitz on the other hand was an entrepreneur and a pragmatist. It is therefore neither useful nor expedient to compare their personalities. Red Bull owes its success to the creative drive and personality of Dietrich Mateschitz and not to the teachings of Viktor Frankl. On the other hand, Frankl supplied the framework of values within which Red Bull really does "give wings" to employees, athletes, and dissenters of all kinds and persuasions, and has done so every day. Many of those who share this approach love Red Bull for precisely this reason. And whenever those who have been indoctrinated criticize, or even show hostility towards the brand, whichever type of "-ism" they may belong to, it strengthens the belief of Red Bull's supporters that they are on the right path.

Conformism is the scourge of our time—we do what everybody does. Nor does it require totalitarian systems these days; indoctrination takes place today more subtly than that, in the filter bubbles and echo chambers of social media. The element of truth in an item of information is no longer a criterion, and en passant the achievements of the Enlightenment are abolished once more. The world is flat; humans have never set foot on the moon; and vaccines transmit Aids—today there is no limit to the range of alternative facts.* The dangerous aspect of this development is that a discussion which should be carried out humanistically, is being politicized, although the dangers lie on all sides. From the self-styled 'liberal' wing, depending on one's point of view, there are the threats of predatory capitalism, the pursuit of success, short-term gains, and a random succession of single brief moments of pleasure in consumption, which allow the protagonist only the choice between hedonism and nihilism. From another perspective,

---

* The networks (Google, Facebook, etc.) react only hesitantly to criticism of this kind. As technology concerns which merely make platforms available, they do not see themselves as responsible for the content users post. For more detail on this subject, see *Zucked: Waking up to the Facebook Catastrophe*. The author Roger McNamee was one of the first investors in Facebook and was a supporter of Mark Zuckerberg, but is one of his most outspoken critics today. Dietrich Mateschitz, who was also critical of these developments and of social media, founded "Quo Vadis Veritas," "Addendum," and "Pragmaticus" as projects which endeavor to produce truthful reporting.

doubts are expressed as to whether we are capable, or whether we should even be allowed, to assume responsibility. They want to protect us from ourselves with rules and regulations which seem increasingly Kafkaesque and which are dreamt up in the protected workshops of trade-union ideals. The nanny state wants to protect us, also—and especially—from ourselves, and to gently but firmly regulate and accompany our fate, from cradle to grave. Also, there is the threat of social convention, compromise, and political correctness.

Thus the general identity crisis proceeds existentially in a "humanitarian" way between heteronomy and self-determination. Seduced, mothered, standardized, and calculated, today—as yesterday—it is not a given to swim against the tide, to find one's specific task in life—and to remain decent in the process. No more and no less.

The experiences in four concentration camps, including Auschwitz and Theresienstadt, taught Frankl that there are only two kinds of people: those who are decent and those who are not. Living according to humanist principles means striving to have the courage for intellectual independence and the development of talents, and to know at the end of one's life, *for what* one has lived. The *why* in any case eludes our imagination. Both Frankl's insights and Red Bull encourage people to do just that—contrary to all social conventions.

May readers be inspired by this encouragement, both in their professional career and their personal life. Frankl's teachings deserve to serve as guides not only in the world of work but also within the family and society. Moreover, by reading this book, readers will not only gain an insight into the history and culture of Red Bull as a company. They will also experience how corporate history, philosophy, and the bold thoughts and actions of individual personalities combined to create a unique, indeed an inspiring, unit. Because Viktor Frankl should be seen not only as the founder of a school of thought which established the component of meaning as the decisive motivation for human activity, and thereby exerted a decisive influence on Dietrich Mateschitz and/or Red Bull. Equally important, and perhaps crucial for coming generations, is that in doing so he laid the foundation for an economy and management philosophy oriented towards meaning, talent, and strengths. In economic theory, the Viennese School around Carl Menger, Ludwig von Mises, and Friedrich August von Hayek builds on these concepts as well as on the management theory of Peter Drucker. The emphasis on the significance of the individual, and his or her contribution to evolutionary creation, originated in Vienna: it opposes the dominant reductionism of the neoclassical theory of a Chicago School as well as the doctrines of a John Maynard Keynes in economic sciences and the process-oriented, dehumanized management of a Frederick Winslow Taylor.

If you like, here a philosophical battle of strength is taking place, with Viktor Frankl as its principal representative. The struggle is between nothing less than a human versus a dehumanized worldview: humanism versus conformism and nihilism, individualism versus automation and process-orientation, selflessness versus personal fulfillment, entrepreneurial flair versus mathematical models of equilibrium, and ultimately the postulate of a free will against a totalitarian and existentialist determinism. The position of Viktor Frankl is: "The decisive element is always the human being. But what is a human being? The being that always decides. And what does it decide? What it will be in the next moment."

I
THE **VALUES SYSTEM** OF VIKTOR FRANKL AND THE **CORPORATE CULTURE** OF RED BULL

// The aimless individual suffers his fate;
the man with an aim shapes his. //
IMMANUEL KANT

Viktor Frankl was a humanist. Humanism is a worldview which respects the dignity of the individual and his or her personality and life. It practices tolerance and champions freedom of conscience and freedom from violence. A humanist ethic affirms life, freedom of choice, and development opportunities. Ideas must be thought of and thought through, but require the unleashing of human strengths in order not to remain figments of the imagination. True adventures do not occur only in the mind, but must become part of real life, must materialize if they are to endure and have significance. Otherwise we shall remain, as Arthur Schopenhauer aptly remarked, merely, "Theater directors of our dreams, [and not] of our own fate." And conversely, our thoughts must be conscientiously examined before we act. While in acting we mostly have to overcome our weaker self, in thinking we must put to one side the "sense-organ" conscience, the "contrary power of the mind." It is not sufficient to be a visionary. Each vision requires a double corrective, namely its feasibility in the real world while preserving the principle of decency. Without this check, visions can also lead straight into ruin. Frankl reminds us that we know "since Auschwitz ..., what man is capable of. And since Hiroshima ..., what is at stake."

For the humanist, humankind and his legacy to the world, his good works, are a starting point but are not the measure of all things. Like Hugo von Hofmannsthal's *Everyman*, individuals faced with their own mortality must give of their best, do good works, and devote themselves to something that is larger than they are. They must surpass themselves. "The crisis of humanism begins where the individual stands in the forefront of observations, and becomes the focus of assessment—the yardstick of all evaluation," wrote Viktor Frankl in *Der leidende Mensch*.*

The external enemies of humanism are totalitarianism and conformism. We must not be deterred from doing what is right by official compulsion or arbitrariness or social expectations. According to Frankl's works it is our conscience that demands that we maintain our inner freedom despite external dependence. Only an individual "who surpasses himself can grow to become himself." Our inner enemies are nihilism and existentialism. They deny a meaning to life; the nihilist practices a lack of responsibility towards himself and society; the existentialist counters a meaningless and hence absurd world with the symbol of Sisyphus, who is forced permanently to roll the stone of tribulation, but whose existence ultimately remains without purpose. Frankl argues against this with the "search for meaning," the value and significance of one's own free actions and one's own contribution to the whole. "Adopt a goal, head towards it, achieve it, and you will become another person. Someone who accepts a challenge goes through life differently from someone who lives aimlessly," he writes.

---

* Viktor Frankl is quoted from the usual editions of his works, lectures and from various websites (see Further Readings in the Appendix). See especially the book *Berg und Sinn. Mit Viktor Frankl im Vorstieg* by Michael Holzer and Klaus Haselböck, published in 2019.

In his books, Frankl is concerned with the central questions of dignity, meaning, and responsibility. His basic thoughts on these concepts will be outlined below. At the same time we shall immerse ourselves more deeply in the world of Red Bull and will show how Dietrich Mateschitz's actions were influenced by these concepts, and how they continue to influence Red Bull to this day. Frankl's search for meaning can be summarized in three concepts that also play a central role for Red Bull: freedom and personal responsibility, the nature of life as a task, and trust and appreciation, together with the method of paradoxical intention. Viktor Frankl's values form, so to speak, the intellectual framework for this narrative and facilitate our understanding for the connections between the two worlds: a task-oriented corporate culture and the principles of a humanist worldview.

1 FREEDOM AND PERSONAL RESPONSIBILITY

*// It is not a disgrace to fail to reach one's goals,
but it is a disgrace not to have a goal! //*

VIKTOR FRANKL

For Frankl, the respect and dignity of the individual are inalienable. To this respect and dignity belongs the conviction that nothing can compel the individual to his fate, neither genes, nor character, nor circumstances. "Instead of despairing that the concrete circumstances of life do not fulfill existing ideas, Frankl recommended that one should respond to these circumstances," it states in *Ärztliche Seelsorge*. Basically, Frankl accomplishes here a "Copernican turn" in the question as to the meaning of life. Individuals have the right and the duty in all situations in life to decide freely and on their own responsibility. We can bring assurance into our own life and the lives of others by means of our free will.

The story with the marble which Frankl narrates in his memoirs *Was nicht in meinen Büchern steht*, shows clearly what Frankl means by personal responsibility for decisions of conscience. Like his brothers and sisters, Frankl also endeavored to acquire an exit visa during the early 1940s. His sister Stella had already succeeded in leaving for Australia with her husband Walter Bondy, and his brother Walter initially escaped with his wife Else to what he thought was a place of safety in Italy. At this time Frankl was working in the Rothschild hospital in Vienna, and he and his parents were accordingly protected from deportation to concentration camp. In the autumn of 1941, Viktor Frankl was granted an exit visa for America, but his parents were not. It was valid for three weeks and plunged him into a severe inner conflict. Should he leave Austria and continue his studies and teaching at an American university, or remain in Vienna? If he left the country, his parents were certain to be deported to a concentration camp, while if he remained he and his family faced an uncertain future in Austria. He thought again about what his decision should be—this time while listening to organ music in St. Stephen's Cathedral, although at the time it was forbidden for Jews to enter the church—and then returned home to Czerningasse 6 in the Leopoldstadt district. He saw a piece of marble lying on the table. His father had found it round the corner, by the destroyed synagogue in Tempelgasse, while out for a walk. The stone was a part of the Tablets of Stone with the Ten Commandments from the synagogue. "A Hebrew letter had been engraved onto the stone. My father said: 'If you are interested, I can tell you which of the Ten Commandments this stone fragment belongs to. Because this letter can only be the first letter of one commandment: Honor thy father and thy mother: that thy days may be long upon the land which the Lord thy God giveth thee.' And in this moment I knew: That was the answer. I allowed the visa to lapse."

Predictably, the decision had severe consequences for Frankl. His young wife Tilly, whom he had met only a short while previously and who was carrying his child, was compelled to have an abortion because Jews were subject to deportation if they became pregnant. The young man could only pursue his beloved hobby, climbing, on rare occasions, and then only at the risk of his own life. To travel to the Mizzi Langer Wall in the Wienerwald without the Star of David on his coat would mean immediate deportation if he ran into a control. A short while later, the Rothschild-Spital was expropriated and repurposed as a military hospital for the SS. Frankl lost his protection from deportation and was deported to the Theresienstadt concentration camp in September 1942 together with his wife, his wife's mother, and his parents. During the following years his entire family with the exception of his sister in Australia were killed in concentration camps.

Viktor Frankl survived not only because he was lucky. In Auschwitz, where he had been transferred in October 1944, he was in the group destined for the gas chamber, but was able to slip over into the other group of younger, stronger men in a moment when he was apparently not being watched. Either the SS guard had failed to notice or had intentionally looked the other way. Frankl already knew from Theresienstadt that decency and political views did not always mutually define each other.

Frankl also survived because he wanted to survive, in order to present his lecture on logotherapy and existential analysis at the adult education college following this "key experiment," as he called it—and he wanted to see his beloved mountains once more. On countless occasions while he was in the camp, he imagined the climbing expedition on the Rax, step by step and handhold by handhold. And so "mountain climbing, the memory of what the rock felt like … became one of the reasons to survive the horrors of the concentration camp." His new life began after he was liberated from Türkheim concentration camp in April 1945.

He embarked on it "step by step—in the same way," and in it he would realize that, "Meaning in life is not only essential, but in this extreme situation is even essential for survival."

Life confronts us all with decisions which we have to take personally and responsibly. We can hope that the circumstances and consequences will not be as dramatic as in Viktor Frankl's case. But the incident with the marble fragment makes it clear that we are called upon, even in the most adverse circumstances, not to become victims of the situation, but to determine our fate ourselves. We are responsible for every moment in our life through our decisions, and the opportunities will be "forfeited" if they are not realized. For Viktor Frankl, life is a novel which is being written in every moment of life. And once something has been entered into the book of life, it can no longer be erased and will remain there—"for all eternity." At the same time, our own future, that of our fellow-humans and the things around us, will be influenced by these decisions, whether they are big or small. "What I achieve through them, what I 'realize in this world,' I am saving in reality and hence am preserving it from transience," wrote Frankl in *Ärztliche Seelsorge*.

The individual is responsible for how he decides, and his behavior will not be constrained by circumstances. Frankl rejects determinism, which would make us believe that circumstances or character, descent, genes, or the compulsion of a situation, dictate human behavior. He pleads for the freedom of individuals to decide and hence to take their fate into their own hands. Freedom and responsibility depend on each other, "Human existence [is] being responsible, because it is being free." And then he writes: "Freedom is not something you have—like something that you could lose;

'I am' freedom." In this respect, Frankl repeatedly suggested in his lectures that, "I recommend that the Statue of Liberty be supplemented by a Statue of Responsibility on the West Coast."

How the foundation for a modern concern was laid in the early years of Red Bull

" We either make our lives miserable and pile obstacles along our path, or we live consciously and clear away the obstacles on the path towards our goal. The amount of work is the same. "

CARLOS CASTANEDA

The founding years of Red Bull were also characterized by free decisions made primarily by a single person as a matter of personal responsibility. Dietrich Mateschitz is, as it were, Red Bull—and vice-versa. Red Bull is his invention and reflects his thoughts and lifestyle. The success gave Mateschitz the freedom "to give people wings", so that they can realize their own ideas.

Mateschitz grew up in the Mürz Valley in Styria. His mother, a primary school teacher in St. Marein, brought him up in line with traditional values. Throughout his entire life he believed in a good upbringing in the sense of modesty, straightforwardness, and good manners. After passing his *Matura* (school-leaving examination) at a boarding school in Graz, he went to Vienna to study at the University of World Trade. "Two or three years longer than I perhaps might have needed," he said of himself. Here he also attended the lectures of Viktor Frankl, with more enthusiasm than some of the other lectures related to his course of study. After completing his studies, which he achieved in 1972 with a degree in business management, he seriously considered emigrating to California to join the group surrounding the writer Carlos Castaneda, but then decided to learn about marketing at Unilever. After a short period of experience in the sales department at Jacobs Kaffee in Austria, he moved to Blendax, where he was employed as the Global Director of Marketing until he founded Red Bull.

The teachings of Viktor Frankl and Castaneda's literary figure, Don Juan Matus, alongside a story-book career in fast-moving consumer goods (FMCG for short)—were two parallel universes, which eventually no longer fitted together. The breakup came after ten years traveling the world for Lever Brothers, during which Mateschitz always organized his routes in such a way that he had enough space to pursue his passions away from business. "It was all too conventional. People in uniform, suit, tie, and all clutching the same newspaper. I said to myself: 'As a Styrian born and bred you don't fit in there.' And then, with it all, a budget with which 'you could do a bit of advertising'," he reported in 2008 in an interview with *Die Zeit*.* Tired of the stories from

---

* Marco Lauer, "Der Illusionskünstler", *Die Zeit*, April 10, 2008, p. 38. Dietrich Mateschitz, it should be noted here, only gave interviews sporadically, and on selected subjects. He refused to appear on television. And Mateschitz was only heard on one brief occasion on the radio, after Red Bull won the Formula One World Championship for the first time. Mateschitz commented, not entirely seriously, that he would give his next interview when Red Bull Salzburg won the Champions League. In his rare public appearances, Mateschitz did not talk about himself, but provided background information about the company and his projects. (Another characteristic was that he never spoke in the first person, either in the media or during other conversations, but only ever in the plural). That corresponded with the principle that Red Bull did not talk to the media, but

the business class, Mateschitz fled from the world of grey suits and founded Red Bull.

The company name was derived from the Thai energy drink Mateschitz often consumed on his business trips to overcome his jet lag and revive himself. His friend and business partner Chalerm Yoovidhva recalled: "Our own company TC Pharmaceuticals and Blendax were business partners. Dietrich came to Bangkok to meet me. He was jet lagged after the long flight from Europe so I offered him a glass of Krating Daeng. It worked. Dietrich's jet leg disappeared and he was regenerated—and impressed." Krating Daeng, translated from Thai as Red Bull, would fundamentally change the lives of the two men.

Red Bull was a sort of place of longing for Mateschitz—a place where the two parallel worlds would fuse. His dreams were ambitious and definitely contrary. From the beginning, the projection surface of Red Bull had clear contours and was to leave behind not only the usual marketing mix, which Mateschitz could produce to perfection in his sleep, but also the limitations of the average civilized population, including the predetermined career leaps with their usual attributes

---

communicated via the media, in other words spread Red Bull content editorially wherever possible. Tina Deutner, who as former assistant of Dietrich Mateschitz coordinated the corporate communication in the company, usually answered requests for interviews with Red Bull employees as follows: "We regret that an interview of this nature is not possible. You—as a long-standing observer of our company—are aware that we work very hard to ensure that the results of our work speak for themselves and thus should be in the foreground; the people who work behind the scenes on our projects prefer to remain behind the scenes." It is understandable but intentional that she did not make herself popular with the media with this comment. Mateschitz set great store by the fact that she always occupied the bottom position in the annual ranking of the best press and corporate spokespersons in Austria.

and status symbols. *Beyond the Ordinary* became the DNA of Red Bull—multi-faceted, diverse, and true to the principles of a life in freedom and responsibility. This world was to include a simple, contemplative hermit's life—one that Mateschitz sometimes led on the beach in Thailand in the hut of his friend and subsequent business partner Chalerm Yoovidhya—as well as extreme experiences like skiing, driving a car or a motorcycle, or complete dedication to the *one* thing. In his case, that was to be the world of Red Bull. Years later, when Mateschitz was sitting in a London taxi on his way to a shareholder meeting with his product in his hand, he said: "It's crazy, but everything we do we owe to this can." And turning to the taxi driver, he added: "Did you know that this can is a once-in-a-century event?"*

The business model behind the can was the positioning of the drink as a luxury and target-group drink, the creation of a completely new communications policy, and the establishment of a global brand with a revolutionary content-marketing concept. All in all, the implementation of a large-scale marketing idea *with a clear mind and open eyes.*

At a time in which people were still speaking of founding companies and start-up capital, the realization of this dream was by no means a matter of course. Far removed from the start-up and venture-capital culture of the twenty-first century, Mateschitz was taking on a huge risk at the age of forty. He followed the dictates of his heart. For the first three years the path he trod was a stony one. Mateschitz

---

* It was the journey by taxi during the course of which he decided to introduce Red Bull Sugarfree, following lengthy internal discussions and against the advice of his marketing department. At the time he had already been consuming a special sugar-free version for many years. It was marked by a colored dot on the bottom of the can.

scraped together all his savings and founded Red Bull in Wiesbaden. For three years he tried to get his energy drink approved in Germany, but the health authorities rejected it with a typical German stubbornness and tenacity. This was despite the fact that, for decades, energy drinks had been sold in their millions in Japan as dietary foods, as so-called over-the-counter (OTC for short) drinks, and accordingly an "epidemiological study of epic proportions" (Dietrich Mateschitz) had taken place there. Taisho, the company that manufactured Lipovitan, the local market leader, was one of the major taxpayers in Japan, a circumstance which—apart from the revitalizing effect of these drinks on long-distance flights—had first given Mateschitz the idea of launching energy drinks in Europe. But at first the authorities were simply not prepared to listen.

These three years were a sort of purgatory, and on more than one occasion Mateschitz saw himself "ending up sleeping under a bridge." They left their mark on Mateschitz's further career, and from then onward his motto was: Do not avoid any battle that is worth fighting, and never give up!

Salvation came in the form of a final injection of capital from his Thai partners and a detour to Austria. In 1987 the Austrian Ministry of Health approved Red Bull with its active ingredients taurine, glucuronolactone, and caffeine, as a dietary food through "non-prohibition". One department of the Ministry of Health had refused approval on the grounds that Red Bull contained potent ingredients and should therefore be classed as a medication, another had simply not seen the need for sugar water containing large amounts of caffeine. Mateschitz had a copy of both these assessments when he demanded that the Ministry decide:

sugar water or medication? Since they were unable to agree whether Red Bull was useless, "expensive" sugar water or a highly potent medication, they came up with a typically Austrian solution: they failed to reply to the application for authorization, and the legal position was that, once three months of non-prohibition of the application had elapsed, Mateschitz could go ahead. The regulatory obstacles were thus overcome for the new drink, thanks to the pragmatic approach of the Austrian authorities, and the starting shot was fired. After three years of enforced desk-top research, the marketing of the drink could begin.

Back then, in 1987, there were not many people who would have placed their bets on the success of Red Bull. The headquarters were established across one hundred square meters in Mateschitz's Salzburg apartment, in the street that leads southwards from the center of Salzburg towards the Alps. He himself moved into a farmhouse on a rise overlooking Lake Fuschl. Together with his assistant Brigitte Aigner, Otto Mattes as Head of Sales, and Robert Hohensinn for night gastronomy, they set out to establish a market where there was none. "First we shall create this market," they announced confidently in the first trade advertisement in *Konsum*. Mateschitz would prove that he was right.

It was not easy at the beginning, however. People in Europe only knew soft drinks: sugar water with artificial coloring and flavorings. The most famous was—and still is—Coca-Cola. If we remember that immediately after the victory of the Allies in the Second World War, Coca-Cola was supplied to the troops with the same degree of urgency as weapons, we can imagine the size of the empire that the firm had built up with the support of the American government, which had also created the legal framework so that Coca-Cola could quickly be sold legally in Europe.

From the mid-1960s, Friedrich Petuely was an influential food expert in Austria, and as such more feared than esteemed. In his function as Director of the Bundesanstalt für Lebensmitteluntersuchung und Lebensmittelforschung (Federal Institute for Food Testing and Research) in Vienna, and as a co-creator of Austrian Food Law, he endeavored in the early 1970s to prohibit Coca-Cola because of the phosphoric acid it contained, or at least to ban the use of caramel syrup as a coloring agent. If Councillor Petuely had prevailed, Coca-Cola would have lost its characteristic brown color. After the American ambassador intervened with the Austrian Federal Chancellor Bruno Kreisky, he abandoned his proposal. Councillor Petuely was later retired with a monthly pension of 55,000 schillings—albeit for other reasons.

We can assume that in other European countries, too, comparable interventions ensured the problem-free sale of Coca-Cola. The United States and Coca-Cola thus achieved after the war within the space of a few months what Red Bull would need decades to achieve: the establishment of a new category of drinks in Europe.

2 THE WILL TO FIND MEANING, OR THE NATURE OF TASKS IN LIFE

// The point is not what we expect from life,
but rather what life expects from us. //
VIKTOR FRANKL

According to Frankl, it is the "search for meaning," that "ultimately permeates the depths of our being." Moreover, it is not only "a specifically human characteristic to ask questions concerning the meaning of life, but it is also an essentially human characteristic to question that meaning." In *Das Leiden am sinnlosen Leben* he writes: "In particular it is the prerogative of young people to demonstrate their maturity by questioning the meaning of life." And elsewhere: "To give something meaning would amount to moralizing. And morals in the traditional sense will soon no longer play a significant role. Sooner or later, in fact, we shall no longer moralize, but we shall ontologize morals—good and evil will not be defined in the sense of something that we should do or should not do, but we shall think that a thing is good if it promotes the fulfillment of the entity assigned and the meaning demanded, and we shall regard those things as evil that inhibit the fulfillment of that meaning. So meaning cannot be given, but must be found."

Just as a psychiatrist or therapist cannot tell a patient what is meaningful, so too can we not prescribe meaning to the work of the individual. Instead, each and every one of us must find meaning, with regard to our specific situation and our possibilities. Frankl writes: "Not only does the task change from one individual to the next—corresponding with the uniqueness of each individual—but also from hour to hour, corresponding with the uniqueness of every situation."

We live in the age of arbitrariness of values and loss of tradition. That is both a curse and a blessing. A curse, because many people are robbed of their home and their orientation, so that they have nothing to which they can cling. The vacuum is increasingly filled by a consumer industry of social media, in which we place ourselves in the center of focus. The striving for happiness is omnipresent, and yet it seems that the more we strive to achieve it, the harder it becomes to be happy. Or, as Viktor Frankl puts it: "The more people chase after happiness, the more they chase it away."

A life that did not have tasks for us to face, in which all our needs were always met immediately, would not bring fulfillment, but would result in profound boredom and infinite emptiness. Frankl calls it an "existential vacuum," in the sense of Kant's "presentiment of a slow death." Deadly boredom will also await us if science should grant us immortality. Immortality makes our actions arbitrary, and we would succumb to lethargy, like *Orlando* in the eponymous novel by Virginia Woolf. Only the awareness that we are mortal and that we shall not live forever on this Earth, makes our actions significant and gives life a flow and a script.

Meaningfulness remains omnipresent for each and every one of us. "The situation does not exist in which life would cease to offer us a possibility of meaning, and the individual does not exist, for whom life has no task waiting to be tackled," writes Viktor Frankl in *Die Sinnfrage in der Psychotherapie*. What is decisive here is that we find meaning only in the form of devotion to a task or a person in which we can forget ourselves. Finding one's self means focusing one's life on something—or on someone—else, to create something or to love someone. That is what makes a job or a vocation so meaningful, and especially when we are young, the world of work is more easily accessible than the love and sacrifice for others.

In *Das Leiden am sinnlosen Leben*, Viktor Frankl vividly shows us clearly the mission-like nature of life, by comparing it with the way the eye perceives things: "Man finds personal fulfillment in serving a cause or loving a person. The more he rises to the task, the more he devotes himself to his partner, the more human he becomes, and the more he becomes himself. So he can really only realize his full potential to the extent that he forgets himself and ignores himself. Is it not like the eye, whose ability to see is dependent on not seeing itself? For when does the eye see anything of itself? Only when it is diseased: If I suffer from cataracts, I see a cloud—and thus I perceive the clouding of the lens. And if I suffer from glaucoma, I see a ring of rainbow colors around the light source—and that is my glaucoma. But the ability of my eye to perceive my surroundings is reduced and impaired to the same extent."

A meaningful life is a life full of purpose. Here Frankl's meaningful self-transcendence differs fundamentally from narcissistic self-fulfillment. Self-transcendence is oblivious to the self, while self-fulfillment is always egocentric. It is the colorful world of the careerists, the eccentric world of egoists, the manipulative world of schemers, and the greedy one of speculators. None of them set the task itself in the center of focus, but only the pleasurable consequences of the fulfillment of the task. Their protagonists strive for money, power, fortune, and recognition, without following the arduous but fulfilling path of devotion to a task. The success and failure of an organization depend on energetically opposing such tendencies on a large and a small scale.

The individual with a task who forgets about himself is immune to almost all aberrations. He is a real blessing for a company. He works independently at his task and does not wait for instructions from his superiors or colleagues. He does not win against others, but by overcoming himself and his limitations. Deception always means for him first and foremost self-deception, because he thinks in the long term and patiently pursues a goal that is worth the effort. He does not have to be motivated, but just not demotivated. Nor does he need motivation training, because he always has his objective in plain view. He does not need to be controlled; he must simply be empowered. He is not greedy, because he does not think first and foremost about money during his work. He is not the type of person who would stop at nothing and he does not scheme because his career is not his prime concern. He does not need a complaints box because he feels no sense of grievance. He does not need a coach, because he knows what he wants. He does not suffer from burn-out, because his work gives him strength and energy. He is never bored, because the task challenges him. And he cannot overestimate himself. Only being preoccupied with oneself leads to the risk of overestimating oneself. Modesty, on the other hand, is proof of the fulfillment of the task without consideration of the self, and of maturity. And that was what Dietrich Mateschitz constantly demanded.

The tasks we fulfill contribute to the big picture and do not benefit ourselves in the first instance. It is the same with the devotion we show towards another person: it benefits others, not ourselves. Ultimately, however, Frankl's concern lies in the balancing act between self-transcendence and self-fulfillment, the "forgetting oneself" and the "not taking oneself too seriously" and the trust in one's own abilities to serve the goal or the person. We use our abilities in order to do something, to achieve a goal, and not so that something can happen. That applies to all circumstances in life. On good days it will require a cheerful tranquility, and on bad ones trust—and on very bad ones, tragic optimism. "The situation is earnest, but not hopeless," the officers in the Imperial and Royal army were wont to report during the First World War. When situations appeared desperate and tragic humor was called for, Dietrich Mateschitz liked to cite Karl Kraus, who changed this to, "The situation is hopeless, but no longer earnest." Neither Frankl nor Mateschitz sees this as an invitation to resignation, however. In the fulfillment of our task we tackle it seriously, try hard, make sacrifices in order to reach a goal. To do this we must sometimes go to the limits of our capabilities—or even beyond—if we wish to surpass ourselves.

The call for modesty and the conscientious fulfillment of our duty seems antiquated and hardly worthwhile in a world in which we are accustomed to subject all important decisions in life to the question as to what the direct advantage will be for ourselves. Power, money, and career lie at the center of our quest for recognition, happiness, and success. The goal maxim varies, but is always self-centered. Without the will to find purpose that ignores the self, our striving will remain a chase after happiness which becomes increasingly elusive, the more we strive to achieve it.

Nonetheless, many people want more money and do much in order to earn it. Money that they will then use to consume the so-called achievements of the affluent society. That this does not make them happy is not only a popular saying; it is also impressively underlined by the list ranking the world's happiest nations, where numerous "poor" countries lie above both the United States and Germany.

Frankl argued against the "consumer society focused on the total satisfaction of our needs" in a lecture on the "Islands of Austerity," which he gave in 1984: "All over the world, people—especially young people—suffer from a feeling of purposelessness. They possess the necessities of life; but they lack a purpose in life which it would be worth living for, continuing to live for." We have to fight for our goals, and we must develop a "tolerance of frustration." That means we must swallow the frustrations and be prepared to wait for the fulfillment of our wishes. We should practice managing without something and sometimes even learn how to sacrifice something we already have. Frankl complains that young people "in their lack of tolerance of frustration ... [are] no longer capable of warding off suffering that can be prevented, and enduring suffering that cannot be prevented."

Frankl sees in sport a modern form of austerity, the way out of the mediocrity trap, the path of the modern warrior. Thus he writes in *Bergerlebnis und Sinnerfahrung:* "The individual who is biologically under-challenged arranges voluntarily, artificially, and intentionally necessities of a higher kind by willingly demanding something of himself, by failing and doing without something. In the midst of prosperity, he brings about crisis situations; in the midst of an affluent society he begins to raise islands of austerity— and precisely here I see the function, not to mention the mission of sport in general and alpinism in particular: they are the modern, the secular form of austerity."

Frankl's great merit in psychotherapy lies in showing that the satisfaction of basic needs and desires does not make people happy and satisfied in the long term. In doing so, Frankl prevails not only over Abraham Maslow's motivation theory of the hierarchy of needs, but also over both the other great Viennese schools of psychotherapy, Sigmund Freud's "pleasure principle" and Alfred Adler's "will to power." According to Maslow, all basic needs must first be satisfied so that the individual can fulfill himself and develop; the individual is only free when he lives in luxury. Freud and Adler reduce human actions to a reaction. For Freud it is the reaction to libido, and for Adler it is the reaction to external circumstances. For Frankl, the individual experiences a sense of purpose through autonomous action.

Frankl strives to "bring the individual to a point where he can advance independently to reach his own tasks, having become aware of his own sense of responsibility, and can find the purpose of life which is no longer anonymous, but rather singular and unique," as he wrote in *Ärztliche Seelsorge*. This sense of purpose consists of a dedication to a task, a goal, the acceptance of a challenge, and not in the preoccupation with one's self, in the satisfaction of needs and the pursuit of power and pleasure. This obliviousness in the devotion to something or someone describes the specific character of the task which comprises life. Satisfaction is achieved when goals are reached; the greater the goal and the effort, the greater the satisfaction. For Frankl the mountaineer, that means: "When I arrive at the Preiner Wand, the *vita aktiva*, the active life, will begin—the life which grasps and tackles—literally 'tackles' the rock."

If we continue thinking about these questions concerning the moral issues, the purpose of life, it will become a question of right or wrong in a dual sense: On the one hand, do we live up to the demands life makes of us, and, on the other, do we remain ethical in doing so?

The first thought, of living up to the demands life makes of us, means dedicating ourselves to something that is greater than we are. The second thought is the question of morals, as to what we should do, because it is good or evil. Freely adapted from Frankl, there are only two "races of humans," the ones who are decent and those who are not;* and this "division into types" runs right through all firms and organizations. Even the conscience of decent people will not always

---

* "There are only two races of people, the decent and the indecent." Frankl experienced individual SS guards in the concentration camp as being decent. A security guard deliberately looked the other way when, upon his arrival at Auschwitz, Frankl tricked his way out from a group of people who were to be gassed to another group. The former concentration camp prisoner Boris Cyrulnik said something very similar in an interview *(Der Spiegel* No. 10 / March 4, 2023): "There were two survivors, one was me"). In 1944, as a six-year-old child, Cyrulnik was sent from Vichy/France to an extermination camp to be transported away. He was able to hide and later save himself in a Red Cross vehicle. "Then a German soldier gave the signal to leave. I still think to this day that he deliberately overlooked me... for me, it really got complicated as a kid after the war was over. Until then everything was clear: All those who hid me were good people, all others were mean Nazis. Then I realized that it's not that simple to deal with the words good and evil. These are in each of us but we tend to shy away from that thought. But if we were to accept this, that would prevent any kind of ideology. It means that other people do not begin on some sort of correct track. Neither do you."

tell them when they are wrong. And even when we have found a sense of purpose, the uncertainty remains as to whether the decision to commit oneself was not ultimately the wrong one.

History is full of misguided ambition. Robert Oppenheimer did not know that his research into theoretical physics at the end of the 1920s in Göttingen would make him a few years later into the "destroyer of worlds." Serving one's country and risking one's life, if not on the battlefield, was for the many volunteers who went to war on behalf of their native land a matter of conscience and a sacred duty. Victory and defeat often decide—retrospectively—on the sense or futility of these heroic deeds and deaths.*

In the face of the uncertainty as to whether we shall be proven right, Frankl demands in *Das Leiden am sinnlosen Leben* that we show more humility. Because "the fact that not even on our deathbed will we know whether our sensory organ, our conscience, was not ultimately the victim of an illusion, also means that one person does not know whether the conscience of the other was perhaps in the right. There can only be one truth; but no one can know whether he himself, or perhaps someone else, is the one who possesses it."

If we wish to shape our fate and not simply suffer it, we must act. And if we act, the question that is always posed is the one about good or bad, truth or lie, right or wrong. Acting the right way means, first of all, acting according to our conscience. But if our conscience deceives us and we recognize that our decision was the wrong one, here too we

---

* As Tom Rachman showed in his novel *The Rise and Fall of Great Powers*, it is an irony of fate that the outcome of almost all wars is decided on the basis of economic framework conditions and is hence predictable.

are responsible for our actions, "without ever having the freedom to sort it out again. Then it is simply a matter of the right attitude, the right approach, and the right attitude with regard to our own guilt is regret."

How Red Bull created a new market without taking itself too seriously ...

" I do the smallest things with the same thoroughness as the biggest ones, and at the same time the biggest things with the same calmness as the smallest ones.*"*

VIKTOR FRANKL

From the beginning, Dietrich Mateschitz pursued the product and marketing concept of Red Bull with tremendous tenacity and perseverance. He did not relax until he had reached his goal, even against great resistance. He was uncompromising when it came to the ingredients, the positioning of the drink, and its approvals in line with food regulations.

During the 1980s, functional drinks like Red Bull were completely unknown in Europe. There was no market for them. Accordingly, the new category "Energy Drinks" was initially seen by many people as rather unreliable. That changed rapidly, however. The marketing strategy, namely that "Red Bull gives you wings," in combination with intensive product sampling, proved to be both effective and successful.

With regard to the marketing, Mateschitz had already been in contact for quite some time with his friend Johannes

"Hansl" Kastner, of the advertising agency of the same name. They had known each other since their student days, and Kastner had also worked for Young & Rubicam and for Unilever before establishing his own agency in 1982. They produced a legendary joint advertising clip in Thailand, in which an elderly Thai man with only a single tooth in his head advertises with his grandchild (as yet still without teeth) for a future generation with healthy teeth—thanks to Blendax. Mateschitz, with no job and virtually no money, approached Kastner. "He said he had a fantastic product idea for which I should create the advertising, but he also had a problem: he could not pay me for it." So Mateschitz worked as a freelance for the agency and created advertising concepts. No fewer than seven were presented to customers, but not a single pitch was won. Kastner remembered that "the concepts were as uncompromising as the way Red Bull is managed today."

From 1984, "Didi and Hansl" spent eighteen months polishing the concept of Red Bull. After months of trials, fifty campaigns, and "countless bad ideas", over which the cooperation threatened to break down—including "Red Bull—Die Freiheit des Adlers" (the Freedom of the Eagle), and a series of advertisements for body and mind, with Schwarzenegger on the right and Einstein on the left*—Kastner finally came up with the exciting idea with the wings slogan, after Mateschitz had asked him to sit down one last time and think. Mateschitz himself remembered

---

* Years later, in fact, Arnold Schwarzenegger would promote the Red Bull World Stunt Award and Mateschitz would launch (unsuccessfully) a "Zweistein" gastronomy and drinks concept with the image of Einstein. Walter Köhler would implement with Terra Mater the Freedom of the Eagle in the film *Brothers of the Wind*, with Jean Reno and Tobias Moretti in the leading roles.

the situation thus: The phone call had come at two in the morning. Of course he had not been asleep at the time; he never needed more than four hours' sleep, "because it only takes up time which you can experience actively." Kastner said: "I've got it." Mateschitz: "So let's hear it." Kastner: "Red Bull verleiht Flügel." ("Red Bull gives you wings.") Mateschitz: "You see! That's what we have been looking for all along."*

Kastner later recalled those exciting times in an interview with the business magazine *trend* on the occasion of Mateschitz's election as "Man of the Year 2001": "We both realized immediately that that was it." The five million schillings with which the two of them made the drink known in Austria, represented "almost his entire own capital. That shows how uncompromisingly Didi believed in advertising. He is a brilliant analyst, but he also has a gut instinct for advertising, a combination that you seldom find together."

Kastner's slogan was then implemented in the unique cartoons of Red Bull. Spots like "Reporter" and "Leonardo" were created primarily as a result of their initial dilemma. Money was short and the cartoons were much cheaper than classic advertising spots. The best supplier of ideas was a policeman from the Mur valley, Mateschitz's home region, and the drawings were produced in Hungary. In that way the campaign was realized for a fraction of the budget of traditional advertising spots. So the dilemma developed into a characteristic campaign with a high recall value. In

---

* The invention of the wings slogan continues to mark the agency to this day. They describe their working method, referring to the traumatic experience of the countless attempts, thus: "All our knowledge and courage in an atmosphere of constructive debate, as a contribution to the customer briefing—overflowing wastepaper baskets until we find the great brand idea ..."

the meantime, even today, thirty years and billions of consumed cans later, hundreds of cartoons are broadcast worldwide. They implement the effect of the product and the brand idea of Red Bull simply, concisely, and humorously, and they still continue to delight the public.

But back to the founding phase: initially Mateschitz was running what today would be described as a start-up. The product: energy drinks as a copycat product from Japan and Thailand. These "blue-collar drinks" are not carbonated and are sold over the counter in little brown bottles as a medicinal product. The well-to-do classes were not interested in these drinks; the target group was the malnourished workers (hence the expression *blue collar*) or lorry drivers who wanted to stay fit and alert. Initially, Mateschitz's greatest concern was whether he would succeed in keeping this product image out of Europe for long enough, so that the energy drinks could become established in Europe as a luxury product for a white-collar target group? The business model was to sell the drink for three times the price of Coca-Cola and thereby to generate a gross profit which would permit the realization of ambitious marketing concepts. And, ultimately, the invention of a new content-marketing concept: brand ambassadors from the world of sport and culture, as well as diverse events, would embody the product idea and make Red Bull famous.

As previously mentioned, the recipe consisted of the ingredients caffeine, taurine, and glucuronolactone. Taurine is a so-called semi-conditional amino acid. As an osmo-regulator, it plays an important role in a number of metabolic functions. Normally, the human body produces sufficient taurine in the adrenal gland, but "in times of increased exertion" it can make sense to take additional amounts of taurine. The caffeine content was increased in comparison with soft drinks; Red Bull contains roughly three times as much caffeine as Coca-Cola. Glucuronolactone aids detoxification. Further ingredients included glucose, saccharose, vitamins, and the characteristic "gummy-bear" flavor from Thailand.

In a survey of a so-called focus group before the product launch, Red Bull was a spectacular failure. The taste was just too gruesome. Mateschitz stuck to his guns. It was not the taste that was crucial, but rather the effect. It was possible to measure the effect both objectively and subjectively. Studies proved that "in times of increased exertion," Red Bull increased performance and improved reaction times and concentration.

For Mateschitz, the recipe and the health-related statements on the can were sacrosanct. During the first years, Roland Concin, who had been the Head of Production responsible for Red Bull at the Rauch filling plant many years before he joined Red Bull as Chief of Operations, changed the production process without authorization. When Mateschitz learned what had happened, he phoned Concin and "came down on him like a ton of bricks". In addition to important health-related statements, the claim "Erhöht die Wachsamkeit" (Increases watchfulness) was to be found on all cans. The food advocate in Germany called Red Bull headquarters in 1996 to inform them that they had been able to reach agreement with the authorities regarding new claims. Amongst other things he had been able to persuade the authorities to agree to the statement "Erhöht die Wachsamkeit" (Increases watchfulness). Although he threatened to resign from his position, Mateschitz let it be known that only dogs were watchful and he insisted on the correct formulation "Wachheit" (Alertness) —which was then adopted.

Mateschitz always insisted that consumers should be allowed to form their own personal ideas regarding the effects of Red Bull as a drink for target groups. Red Bull is adequately positioned with the slogan "Verleiht Flügel" ("Gives You Wings") and the reason why "Belebt Geist und Körper" ("Vitalizes body and soul"). This enables everyone to project onto the drink the effect that he or she finds most important. One person may value the enhanced performance in sport, while others are looking for a pick-me-up at work or in their leisure activities. Red Bull is also popular as a stimulant when driving long distances, or as a party drink that is reputed to make you alert and yet able to hold your drink.

Incidentally, it is only the consumption of a full 250-milliliter can of Red Bull that will produce the desired effect. Accordingly, Red Bull is not available for "tasting" in a plastic beaker in the supermarket like a soft drink. The cans are always distributed by so-called *Wings Team Members* to consumers when Red Bull is required in order to get through the day or the night alert and in good spirits. The cans are opened before they are handed over, so that they can actually be consumed on the spot and "in times of increased exertion." The effects of Red Bull should be noticeable, and that will only be the case when you really need some extra energy.

Generations of marketing people at Red Bull have to be convinced time and again that they should allow the consumer his or her own subjective idea of the effects of the drink. That was not always easy—and the problem remains to this day. Many a brand manager, newly recruited from the major FMCG concerns, has wanted to position the product more precisely, for example as a sports drink, which would limit the potential of Red Bull to that of Isostar or Gatorade. Or they want to place a full-page advertisement which lists why Red Bull is not bad for your health; time and again, the idea that it is "not good for me" is named as one of the reasons for not consuming the drink. In the best case, it would be suggested that a customer would be paying three times as much for a Red Bull, which contains no more caffeine than a decent cup of coffee. In the worst case, those consumers who like Red Bull would be put off by the negative message.

From the beginning, countless urban myths grew up around the drink. Amongst these was that it supposedly contained as much caffeine as twenty cups of coffee. Another myth was that the ingredients led to cardiac arrhythmias and in serious cases to a heart attack. It was also said that if it was mixed with alcohol, you would be inebriated but would feel as if you were sober. Resourceful scientists, never embarrassed when it was a question of a research grant, even invented the technical term to describe the "wide-awake-drunk" syndrome. In the early years, the warning "do not mix with alcohol" was even printed on the cans in Austria. Of course, the mainly youthful consumers saw this as nothing less than an invitation, and from time to time a Red-Bull-and-vodka, affectionately known as a *Flügerl* ("Little Wing"), found its way across the bar counter, not in spite of but rather because of the health warning.

Over the years, Red Bull increasingly succeeded in taking the place of Coca-Cola. Fifty years ago, children were forbidden to drink Coca-Cola, which was said to be something for adults only. (It was not for nothing that the stimulating effect of the soft drink was originally due to the addition of cocaine). Now it was Red Bull that parents banned their children from drinking. This parental support ensured that young people of every generation were in a fever of impatience until they were finally allowed to buy their first Red Bull.

In general, health warnings of that kind together with the obligatory media echo increased the attention paid to the product and its category. And they were seen as being exactly what they actually were, namely government advertising. As long as the name Red Bull was correctly written and the sale of the product was not actually prohibited, it was the best thing that could possibly happen to the new brand. Accordingly, Dietrich Mateschitz saw all these phenomena unperturbed and with humor. In 1995, when he was awarded the title of "Marketer of the Year" within the framework of the Effie Gala, and journalists asked him during the awards ceremony whether it was true that taurine was extracted from bulls' testicles, Mateschitz gave the quick-witted reply: "Yes, but only from the testicles of the strongest and bravest animals."

The foundation was laid. Mateschitz knew that the effectiveness of Red Bull could be demonstrated both subjectively and objectively. Following its market launch in Austria, the repeat purchasing rates were high. This was no surprise for Mateschitz, who knew from his own experience how effective energy drinks were. On his countless trips to Asia, the drinks had always helped him to overcome his jetlag.

... And finally conquered the world from its base in Austria

"All we really need is to be allowed to get on with our work in peace."
DIETRICH MATESCHITZ

The little blue-and-silver can bearing the name Red Bull set out on its successful campaign. After three years spent attempting to launch the product in Germany, the success story that would revolutionize the global drinks market within just a few years began in Austria.

During the early 1990s, Mateschitz established Red Bull very successfully in Austria. Everyone was talking about the energy drink. The turnover and profits of a company with just eight employees reached a sensational € 130 million. The product was still not authorized in Germany, so the expansion there took place "via smugglers' routes." Flight attendants and students supplied the aspiring market with the popular party drink that German guests had learned to like and appreciate during their last ski or summer holiday "across the border."

Mateschitz wondered whether he should retire into private life and just act as a shareholder. He appointed a managing director. But by 1994, the short guest appearance of a certain Mr. Vogel was over and Mateschitz, now aged fifty, took firm hold of the reins once more. Once again, he had made a decision freely and as an act of personal responsibility in the sense of Frankl. He did not want to wait until, perhaps, Coca-Cola took serious notice of Red Bull, made a takeover bid, and would then roll out the new category globally. He was going to try it himself. That was a very bold decision for an admittedly highly profitable but very small firm from Salzburg, Austria, that was "marketing small fry" and that had outsourced the production of the cans to Rauch in Nüziders, Vorarlberg. Others can carry out the production better, said Mateschitz, and he would be proved right. Rauch celebrated the centenary of its founding in 2019, and if there is something Rauch can do, it is produce drinks. So why saddle oneself with that task, when Red Bull was out to conquer the world.

In 1993, Red Bull went on sale in Hungary, the first country outside Austria. A sales structure was built up at short notice in the style of the Austro-Hungarian monarchy, and then everything went very quickly. Austria joined the European Union in 1995. In 1994, Red Bull was approved in the UK, which generally adopted a liberal approach in the approval of foods. It was then imported via the UK and through the free movement of goods to Germany. As a market, Germany is ten times larger than Austria, and the flight attendants and students had done quite a lot of the preliminary work. Red Bull was absorbed there like water by a dry sponge. The sales success brought the little team, which had hitherto led a relatively quiet life in the seller's market Austria, into difficulties. A few weeks after the market launch of Red Bull in Germany, Rauch ran out of cans. No one had expected such sales quantities and made plans accordingly. Red Bull was not able to deliver the product, and the shelves remained empty. The trade term for this is OOS—Out of Stock. An attempt to save the day by using glass bottles failed completely because consumers rejected them. It would take Red Bull years to recover in Germany. To this day, the development in Germany continues to lie well behind that of Austria and Switzerland.

For Mateschitz, it was a wake-up call that he would need to put the organization on a more professional footing. From the early 1990s, Anja Köstlinger from the personnel consulting firm Neumann Personalberatung approached dozens of up-and-coming marketing and sales staff, especially at Procter & Gamble, but also at Johnson & Johnson, Unilever, and Kraft Suchard, in order to win them over for Red Bull. Positions in Finance, Operations, and Legal Affairs were either created or refilled. Many employees from this phase of international expansion when the staff numbers were still in the low double figures, were still working for Red Bull in a senior capacity at the time of this publication (over thirty years later).

At this point in time, Red Bull had long since outgrown the apartment in Alpenstrasse. The headquarters of this concern had been moved to Fuschl am See. There, beside the main road and a stone's throw from the southwestern shores of one of the loveliest lakes in the Salzkammergut lake district, a workshop building that had been built by a firm that made baths and taps, was looking for a new owner. Craftspeople were to have been housed in half a dozen bunks, with a workshop and sales under one roof. When the concept collapsed, Mateschitz grasped the opportunity, converted the rooms into offices, and built a meeting and encounter area in the hall between foliage plants and round white stones which bore testimony to the last Ice Age, ten thousand years ago.

The early times in Fuschl sound absolutely idyllic. Mateschitz liked to go surfing at the bathing beach, and if it was a nice day and the work situation permitted it, the staff were allowed to do the same. There were no hierarchies. Instead of superiors, managers, and a back office there were the positions Head Coach, Quarterback, and Defensive Line, following the pattern of American football teams. At lunchtime they all sat at a table in the Mohrenwirt inn and dined à la carte. Nobody bothered about benefits in kind. Everyone—including Hedi Litzlbauer, who cleaned the offices at the time, as a permanent employee, of course—went home in a company car. And yet, in the following years it was here that the course was set for the international rollout of the Red Bull brand.

Mateschitz was a marketing professional. He knew all about the theory. But what would really work in the world out there? The great unknown factor in those days was above all: would the approach that had been successful in Austria also work in other markets? There were no reference figures for the markets outside Austria, and the first results from the new countries were conflicting. In countries like Switzerland and Belgium the concept established itself immediately, but the UK team initially declared categorically that the transcription of the slogan "Red Bull verleiht Flügel" into "Red Bull Gives You Wings" did not even approximately convey what the German version embodied. A classic "Not Invented Here" syndrome. Mateschitz was sceptical, but allowed the English team to pursue their own approach. Eighteen months and considerable losses later, the experiment with the slogan "Never Underestimate What a Red Bull Can Do For You" was brought to a halt, the team was changed, and the content-marketing concept that had proved itself in Austria with the slogan "Gives You Wings," the reason-why statement "Vitalizes Body & Mind," and the cartoons, was launched in the UK as well. And, surprise, surprise, it worked there too.

From this time the conviction grew that that concept could also be successful on a global scale. The prerequisite was a single brand and central marketing coordination based in Fuschl am See, which was increasingly becoming transformed into a proper headquarters. The marketing was directed from the Brand, Sport, Events, Culture, and Communications departments. Local color, as long as it fitted the brand image, was expressly desirable, and the best ideas from the various countries were adopted. Red Bull was materializing as a global brand.

But first of all, the product had to be authorized in the various countries. Theoretically there was free movement of goods within the European Union. But the individual countries had different ideas as to exactly what that meant. In Germany, it had to be proved beyond doubt that the product was not harmful to health, but Brasserie du Pêcheur beer from Alsace that was not brewed according to the German purity law could only be sold following a judgment by the European Court of Justice. That was in 1996, after the brewery had gone through an authorization process in Germany that had lasted for eight years. Based on that standard, the authorization of Red Bull in Germany in 1994 was a success. The authorizations in Belgium, Luxembourg, The Netherlands, Ireland, and Spain also took place largely without complications and according to plan.

There were problems in Italy, the Scandinavian countries, and especially France. Italy suddenly gave up its resistance in 1997 after a statement by the Supreme Health Council. France and the Scandinavian countries fought to the bitter end. The authorization was preceded by a fierce battle between Red Bull and the authorities; the prohibition was maintained for reasons that were constantly changing. Initially, the authorities were displeased at the increased caffeine content. Increased caffeine consumption through energy drinks can, it was alleged, lead to dizziness, restlessness, concentration difficulties, and aggressive behavior. Curious, when we remember that Red Bull contains as much caffeine as a good cappuccino, and cola and iced tea are consumed in large quantities and thereby contribute the lion's share of people's total caffeine consumption. Mateschitz was accordingly acquitted in criminal proceedings brought against him and the French Managing Director Markus Krebs in the Palais de Justice on the Île de la Cité in Paris. That was in early 2000—and the champagne corks popped in Fuschl. Sales could go ahead in France. Or so they thought. They had not reckoned with the tenacity of the French authorities.

Only a few days later, the French Health Council issued a new safety assessment. This time, the ingredients taurine, glucuronolactone, and possible interaction of the individual ingredients were criticized. That meant that the acquittal was invalid. As the legal Latin maintained, it was now a *Nova Producta*—and the second round in the authorization battle could begin. Several more rounds were to follow.

Before they could even think of an authorization for France, it was first necessary to break down the political resistance. France was supported in its scientific committees by the Scandinavian countries and Germany. In Germany, the opposition in the conflict was more nuanced and the attitude to Red Bull could certainly be described as schizophrenic. The fundamentalists at the Federal Institute for Risk Assessment were politically motivated, and saw a connection between energy drinks and a small number of deaths (an attitude they maintain to this day), albeit with the caveat that "a causality ... however has not been proved without doubt to date." Nonetheless, Red Bull was permitted there—in contrast to France. Therefore, while in France nobody believed that it represented a health risk and Red Bull was excluded from the market for political reasons, in Germany the situation was the exact opposite. In the end, Scandinavia referred to France and hoped that the Gallic village would remain impregnable. Austria was delighted at the export surpluses in the rest of the world, but otherwise did not lift a finger. Most of the support came from the UK, which has unfortunately turned its back on the EU since then. We shall miss it. But that's Europe.

The real cause of the problem was not Red Bull and its ingredients, but the French national nutrition policy, which aims at a healthy, (vitamin-rich) balanced diet as early as school. Authorizing Red Bull would have been tantamount to an admission of complete failure. France had to prevent the undermining of decades of unavailing efforts for as long as possible, and even against the rules of free movement of goods. The authorities were used to dealing with large concerns like P&G, Unilever, Coca-Cola, and Pepsi, which took that into account, adapted, and modified their recipe to suit the market in question. So why shouldn't little Red Bull from Austria do the same?

That might be a viable approach for manufacturers of cereals and soft drinks, but for Red Bull it was not. Dozens of studies on the effectiveness of the functional foodstuff would have been obsolete and useless, and the consumer would have justifiably posed questions about the original recipe in other countries and the effectiveness of the watered-down product.

As so often, here Red Bull sought agreement and not a compromise. Further time-consuming individual and interaction studies would have to be commissioned. Interaction studies in particular were completely unknown in the case of foods, and were only carried out for medicines when the metabolization of individual active ingredients gave cause to speculate about drug interaction. In the case of the ingredients of Red Bull, there was no reason to expect interaction of an additive, inhibiting, or synergistic nature, and accordingly the studies that were demanded were of no use. But in most cases the authorities were concerned not with consumer protection, safety concerns, and the overworked 'precautionary principle,' which they even admitted off the record, but rather with a matter of nutrition policy, prevention, and—if Red Bull could not be stopped—at least delaying tactics. Meanwhile, Red Bull had engaged Robert Kroes, Andrew Renwick, Ron Walker, and Joe Rodricks, the crème de la crème of European and American toxicology and metabolism research: experts who were otherwise busy with the real problems facing humankind, such as—for example—the highly topical safety assessment of "mad cow disease" (bovine spongiform encephalopathy). The scientists were in agreement: Red Bull was harmless. On a political level, scientific pseudo-arguments were used as an excuse and a proxy war was being fought. No serious scientist genuinely believed it posed a health risk, which was why they reacted with increasing irritation to this waste of resources.

After countless studies regarding chronic and acute consumption, as a single ingredient or combined effects as well as metabolic investigations, the European Food Safety Authority (EFSA) passed a statement about taurine and glucuronolactone on February 12, 2009: "two ingredients which are frequently used in certain energy drinks." After this statement, even the last strongholds gave up their resistance to Red Bull. Following the statement, the *Direction générale de la concurrence, de la consommation et de la répression des fraudes*, DGCCRF for short, had no choice but to confirm Red Bull's harmlessness and to allow it also to be sold legally in France. Shortly afterwards, Norway and Denmark followed the French decision, as was to be expected. This was, however, within the framework of a WHO/FAO meeting in Berlin shortly beforehand, where the person responsible in Denmark had informed the author while they were waiting in the lunch queue, that Red Bull would be granted an authorization in Denmark "only over [her] dead body." Fortunately her retirement was all it took instead.

So now, only Germany remained a politically motivated opponent. Even after the EFSA statement in 2009, an attempt was made to prove the damaging effect of Red Bull during sports, or if it was mixed with alcohol. They referred to the precautionary principle, admittedly without taking the logical step of banning Red Bull from the shelves. Studies financed by taxpayers were to confirm the suspicion before that happened. A study was commissioned from the University of Hohenheim, with the aim of proving that the acute consumption of Red Bull led to circulatory and cardiac problems. After the results of the study were presented, EFSA finally stated in 2015 that even "the acute consumption of an energy drink does not influence blood pressure any more than that which would be expected from the consumption of caffeine." In short, the effects of caffeine had been studied at the taxpayers' expense. Any further interactions were not to be expected, and none were discovered. Mateschitz therefore stated correctly that "Red Bull has a better toxicological documentation than some medicines." And so the authorization of the product in Europe was essentially complete after more than twenty years.

The authorities in Australia, New Zealand, and Canada, to name only the most important countries, had already confirmed the harmlessness of Red Bull. In Australia, too, the authorization succeeded only as a result of the free-trade agreement with New Zealand. Several attempts via the food safety authorities in Sydney had previously failed. However, New Zealand had already authorized Red Bull as a dietary food product, as in Austria. Studying the Trans-Tasman Mutual Recognition Agreement, TTMRA for short, during a flight from Auckland to Sydney, led to the breakthrough in Australia. Chris Preston, a lawyer who until recently had been employed by the authority, had become a freelance and he confirmed in a statement that dietary foodstuffs were also covered by the agreement. The Australia-New Zealand Food Authority, ANZFA, gave up its objections. At the end of the 1990s, Red Bull was also shipped to Australia, initially via a stopover in New Zealand ports.

The introduction in the United States posed no problems from a legal point of view. In 1997, Mateschitz decided to launch Red Bull there too. First of all, it was necessary to agree a delimitation agreement regarding the trademark with Stroh, or rather Pabst Brewery. Pabst sells a Red Bull strong beer in the United States. Red Bull even sold the beer, which was well ahead of the times, in Austria for a while, until they realized the pointlessness of the project.

For the United States, one of the prerequisites was a so-called self-affirmation of the ingredients taurine and glucuronolactone. This certification is generally carried out by experts nominated by Red Bull who were recognized by the Food and Drug Administration (FDA). Like almost everything in America, the process was expensive and time-consuming, but eventually pragmatic and successful. The FDA and the Federal Trade Commission (FTC) did not contradict the assessment, and there were no objections to Red Bull as a food product with increased caffeine content.

So energy drinks were also accepted, after coffee and cola. From the point of view of the FDA, probably the last category of foods which were permitted to be enriched with caffeine in large quantities. The authorities would look critically at subsequent caffeine innovations. Thus alcoholic instant caffeine drinks, so-called Alcoholic Mixed Energy Drinks (AmED), were virtually removed from the market by a Warning Letter from the FDA. We can assume that other foodstuffs like water or chewing gum with a relevant caffeine content could count on considerable resistance from the authorities. Coffee, cola, and energy drinks thus remain the main sources of caffeine for the American consumer, apart from the authorization of medicines, a decision which was important for the new category of energy drinks. The last land to authorize Red Bull was Uruguay, in 2014. The global authorization of the product was thus complete.

3 ESTEEM, CONFIDENCE, AND TRUST

" Trust is the great remedy for the emotional distress of our time. "

VIKTOR FRANKL

"If we take people only as they are, then we make them worse. If we treat people as they ought to be, we help them become what they are capable of becoming," according to Goethe's *Wilhelm Meister's Apprenticeship.* Nothing was further from Frankl's mind than to objectify the individual, to reduce him or her to a "nothing but": nothing but nerves, muscles, and tissue; nothing but a product composed of fears, neuroses, environmental conditions, and a genetically predetermined character. Nothing makes this attitude clearer than the allegory Frankl told during a lecture to students in Australia.* He described his flying teacher, who explained to him, when he acquired his pilot's license at the age of seventy, that in the case of a side wind he should steer in the opposite direction and that he would have to shift his imaginary goal—in his example, towards the north, in other words towards the top of the blackboard, in order to reach his chosen destination.

It was no different with people: we must take them as what they could be and not as what they are. Or, as

---

* It was the lecture during which he humorously characterized his distinctive Austrian accent as follows: "I know I am speaking a marvelous accent without the slightest English."

Dostoevsky said: "To love someone means to see them as God intended them."

That is not a naive faith in the good in people, nor is it a set of instructions for positive thinking in the sense of optimistic partiality. To think positively becomes a cognitive distortion if it is unfounded and as an error of confirmation blocks out the information that does not fulfill one's own expectations.* What Frankl means is the opposite of nihilism: not to surrender to circumstances and fate, but to believe unconditionally that individuals are free to form their fate as they choose. He asked appropriately in a lecture: "How should someone who believes that his fate is sealed, be able to overcome it?"

Frankl reveals his humanist worldview in these two fundamental attitudes: to value the individual absolutely and to have confidence—indeed, even to expect—that in any situation he or she will be able to determine their fate as their conscience demands.

The better person needs our goodwill, our trust, and our optimism so that he will make the best out of his abilities.

To take people as what they could be, correspondingly means above all, to have confidence in them. To have confidence in their development potential. To have confidence in the willingness to increase this potential. But above all, the mutual trust that people mean each other well. For Frankl ultimately, trust is "the great cure for the mental distress of our times."

---

* In her eminently readable book *Bright-sided: How the Relentless Promotion of Positive Thinking Has Undermined America,* Barbara Ehrenreich demonstrates by means of recent American history with its widely held *Yes-We-Can* basic attitude that this approach is tantamount to self-deception and leads to mass illusion.

Nothing affects the working environment, moreover, more than trust. The economist Fredmund Malik determines in his book *Managing, Performing, Living* that you can do everything right, manage according to the textbook, set targets, organize, control, and nonetheless the working atmosphere in the department or company can be abysmal. And on the other hand there are executives who do everything wrong according to the textbook, and nonetheless their departments are a stronghold of satisfied employees with a high degree of creativity and productivity. If there is no trust, measures to promote corporate culture and motivation often have the opposite effect and are experienced by the staff as "dishonest, and manipulative as a particularly sophisticated form of cynicism." Or, as Peter Drucker, the American economist with Austrian roots, aptly put it: "Culture will eat strategy for breakfast."*

Little has survived with regard to Frankl's values in his dealings with his members of staff—values which "you cannot teach, but can only live by example." In the Viktor Frankl archives we find, however, a few helpful comments on the subject of trust in the working environment. Thus he said on the occasion of an interview for *3M* from 1972 (let us remember that it was at this time that Mateschitz was just completing his studies): "But perhaps I may make an observation here, if you will allow me: After all, I had been the director of the Polyclinic in Vienna for 25 years, and if

---

* The Austrian economist was born in Vienna in 1909 as the son of an upper-class Jewish family. He is regarded as one of the most influential management thinkers of all times. "Management by Objectives", MbO for short, can be traced back to him. His books were burned in Germany in 1933. As part of the "brain drain" of the Viennese intelligentsia to the New World, he went initially to New York and then to Claremont Graduate University near Los Angeles.

you ask me, describe me so to speak as an amateur, how I treated my staff, then, looking back, I must say that I adopted two principles and made them my own: First of all, I always attempted to make my staff feel that they were specialists in their field just as much as I was in my more specific specialist field, and that it was mere chance, as it were, that I was in charge, and not they. It could equally well have been the other way round. And secondly, I taught them in good time that there was really only one thing with which they could really impress me, only one thing that would really put them in my good books, and that was always and at all times to dare to tell me the critical truth to my face, not to spare me their criticism, because ultimately I was dependent on it."

What Frankl was addressing here were two principles, without which there can be no appreciative and trusting cooperation. In the first lies not only the evident esteem for the employee as an individual, but also that special culture, which makes it possible for success to be celebrated together. Nothing is more conducive to a trusting cooperation than to say at the right moment, "*We* did it," and nothing is more detrimental than to use an *I* in the wrong place and at the wrong time, when really a plural or even the third person, that is, a *we*, a *he* or a *she* would have been appropriate. We can derive a handful of simple rules from all this: the mistakes of the superior remain his mistakes alone, and the success of the employee is always his success alone. The employee's mistake is always also the mistake of the superior, and the success of the superior is generally the success of the whole department.

The second principle, to tell the boss the truth, demands two things: his willingness to listen and the courage to stand up for something to the best of one's knowledge and belief. Without the integrity of both protagonists, a conversation of this nature will not take place, for the employee must be able to have confidence that his superior will take the information into consideration seriously and, if he believes it would be right to do so, then also act accordingly. If he does not do that, his integrity will be compromised. And on the other hand, the superior must have confidence that the employee will tell him the truth, or at least what he believes to be the truth—in other words that he honestly means it. If he fails to do this, he probably only wants to scheme against someone, or is acting for political motives and then he will lose his integrity. Without the integrity of both protagonists, therefore, there can be no trust. But if there is trust, they will already have achieved a great deal.

Ultimately, without authenticity there can be no trust. And so interventions aiming to change the personality, whether through training course or coaching, are as useless as they are dangerous. We cannot make a cooperative manager out of an authoritarian one, and vice-versa. Managers have tasks to fulfill, not roles to play, which is why their personal management style is of secondary importance, as long as they act authentically. And conversely, there can be no trust where task fulfillment and achievement do not stand in the foreground, but rather connections or intrigues, and where hyper-reflection, in other words the permanent preoccupation with oneself, a determination to control and plan everything, prevents any form of listening.

If a trusting culture dominates in a relationship or an organization, all obstacles can be overcome. Conversely, without it, all efforts will be in vain. It is therefore not surprising that "in excellent firms what will be sensed above all [is] respect for the individual. This basic attitude is omnipresent. Treat people like adults and treat them like partners. Treat them with dignity and respect. Do not treat them like investments or machines, but as the prime source of [creativity, innovation, and consequently also of] increased productivity."* These companies give their employees not only the chance to influence their fate themselves, but they expect it of them. They give people a sense of purpose and thus enable them to achieve "extraordinary results with ordinary people" (Fredmund Malik).

How Red Bull set the parameters for a wealth of ideas and creativity

// If you want to build a ship, don't drum up the men to gather wood, divide the work and give orders. Instead, teach them to yearn for the vast and endless sea. //

ANTOINE DE SAINT-EXUPÉRY

As we have seen, Red Bull progressed to become a global brand and the company increasingly developed into a concern. Being an organization that over the years produced double-figure growth, in some years as much as thirty, sixty or even one hundred percent, resulted in its own particular challenges, and thus work progressed feverishly at headquarters on the organization of the ups and downs of the process, in order to manage with businesslike care the

---

* Thomas J. Peters / Robert H. Waterman, *In Search of Excellence: Lessons from America's Best-Run Companies*, Collins Business Essentials, 2006.

modifications to the organization that became constantly necessary. An ideal organization for small, medium-sized, and large countries was drawn up. Mateschitz insisted on transparent organizations and shallow hierarchies.

In his view, it was the managing directors in the countries who were responsible for the brand development and turnover. The first eight years in Austria served as a reference for this. During this time, he launched Red Bull and made it successful with a handful of employees and partners. The planning as regards content and quality was to take place at a country level, "bottom up" with the marketing measures necessary to build a strong brand, which forms the basis for growth in revenues. Mateschitz rejected a company that was planned purely "top down," of the kind frequently found in publicly listed companies. Red Bull is a company that is controlled with regard to content via the right tasks and which does not administer people and key financial figures. The main focus is on ideas, not maximum profit.

Confronting the strong country organizations is a central management with a Board of Directors whose function is to bear the final responsibility. If on very rare occasions no agreement could be reached between the countries and the Board, or within the Board itself, Mateschitz made the final decision. Headquarters were responsible for strategic planning (Mateschitz) and international coordination, mainly of course by Marketing and Sales. Finance and Operations were also controlled primarily from Headquarters, and Legal Affairs and Human Resources were also classic executive departments within the concern. Mateschitz thereby followed intuitively the Viable System Model of Stafford Beer for effective organizations. As already indicated, production was outsourced to Rauch, and production planning took place in Fuschl.

The finance department was responsible for the classic segments, whereby financial planning and controlling at Red Bull were deeply involved in the business processes. It quite frequently happened that the predictions based on the experience and cautious approach of long-standing CFO Walter Bachinger corresponded more closely with reality than the sales plans of the line. Therefore financial planning made a considerable contribution to the predictability and stability of the concern, not only in the period of expansion.

In the area of process organization, planning and production cycles were laid down, business planning, the First Revised Estimate and Second Revised Estimate established, and SAP introduced. Specimen contracts for sales and the most important business processes were drawn up. The reporting system and bookkeeping followed, in line with the internationally recognized and standardized regulations International Financial Reporting Standards (IFRS) and Generally Accepted Accounting Principles (GAAP). Red Bull is proud that the Annual Financial Statement is always available by mid-January.

Is it an irony of fate that over the years what has developed is precisely what Mateschitz had escaped from in the mid-1980s: a global concern with strict rules and regulations? Or is there still a difference between Red Bull and other major concerns—a specific Red-Bull DNA? And if so, what is its secret?

What was and would remain unique to Red Bull at this time was without doubt Mateschitz himself. Mateschitz was an entrepreneur through and through; he created and pursued his goals with tenacity, determination, and single-mindedness. In doing so, he left nothing to chance. "Red Bull was not a test balloon, but was carefully planned from the very beginning," he said in 2008 in an interview with *Die Zeit*. He was a mover and shaker, said the former mayor of Salzburg. He had an unerring instinct, and "when he had seen that something was right, he would follow it through," commented star chef Eckart Witzigmann. Friends called him "Didi," but within the company the "big boss" was known by his initials "DM". He spoke informally to his closest staff members, but even after working in the firm for decades, they never failed to address him with respect. And whenever he nonetheless adopted a more formal tone when speaking to someone, they knew immediately that he did not agree with something.

Mateschitz had confidence in himself and his abilities; he worked indefatigably, even obsessively, with his goal before his eyes. Like all good entrepreneurs, he believed above all that he could change circumstances positively and in his favor. From the start, he saw the opportunities and possibilities for himself and Red Bull, and not the obstacles and problems. As a result of this approach, Red Bull is basically a solution-oriented concern, and if we were to speak of the firm's aim, it would be always to change things for the better. In doing so, boundaries are literally being shifted permanently.

The path of the warrior that is oblivious of the self, according to Carlos Castaneda, is above all also a path towards independence. Mateschitz loved independence. In himself and in others. He demanded of himself and his surroundings an independence from the weaker self, from all weaknesses, doubts, and moods, in line with Viktor

Frankl's motto "that no one needs to put up with everything about yourself." And at the same time, maximum independence from others, from money from the banks, employees in trades unions who wanted participation in management without assuming responsibility, and independence from the bureaucratic hurdles of politics and administration.

In spite of his growing success, Dietrich Mateschitz retained his conservative values and never lost his down-to-earth attitude. For him, money and power were never an aim in themselves, but always only a means to an end. In the foreground were not maximum profits, but tasks and goals which were pursued consistently. In financial matters, Red Bull still operates carefully and conservatively. Money that has not yet been earned cannot be spent. This attitude is dictated not by narrow-minded parsimony or greed of gain, but guarantees the independence described above. Not profits, but scope of action will be maximized by this attitude. At Red Bull, money is not acquired by saving but by consistently re-investing in the brand and the concern. The global expansion was financed through profits that remained within the concern, not with foreign capital. Money that has already been earned and is thus available is used generously. The global marketing activities cost a great deal of money. "But money is there so that you can do something with it," observed Mateschitz. He did not like to be constantly questioned as to how much something had cost. When questioned about the costs of Formula One, Mateschitz commented: "Money must not be allowed to become a consideration when you have a goal to reach." This approach is not an expression of lack of caution and restraint but his determined will to achieve success, which one can and must afford. Admittedly, the rule also applies that if you achieve success, the profits will generally follow. Therefore, "true thrift never forgets that it is not always possible to make savings," according to Theodor Fontane; "Those who always want to save are lost, also morally." On the other hand, we must never forget that it is a thousand times more difficult to sell something than to buy something and spend money.

The willpower and the creative drive with which Dietrich Mateschitz defended his point of view never failed to charm his opposite number. However, it was not only his natural and invariably appreciative authority that made him a respected figure, but also his equanimity and aplomb. A calm approach played an important role in the world of Dietrich Mateschitz. He was as suspicious of those who never talk about anything but work as he was of those actionists who are permanently stressed and under pressure to perform as they rush from one obligation to the next. A calm approach helps us to tackle apparently trivial tasks with the same diligence as important ones. Viktor Frankl and Dietrich Mateschitz also shared this secret of success: carrying out minor tasks with the same thoroughness as the most important ones, and the biggest challenges with the same calm approach as the smallest ones. Whether a question of the positioning of the Red Bull logo on a sports helmet or the structuring of our sales channels in the United States, by far the largest market with sales of four billion cans in 2022, Mateschitz would listen patiently and attentively and make his decision with the same care. He would not procrastinate, closed gaps in foreseeability with experience and increased consideration, and assumed responsibility for his decisions.

You could also describe this equanimity as remoteness, a conscious distance maintained between people and tasks.

Mateschitz refused to be carried away by ad-hoc opinions and actions. He stood back, first formed his opinion by stopping to think, and perhaps by discussing things with one or the other of those involved. In this way he would often succeed in implementing the idea in the very moment in which it had matured and taken shape.

Mateschitz cultivated what I would call a cooperative-authoritarian leadership style. He always endeavored to include competent and relevant opinions and to reach a consensus. When that was not possible, he would not attempt to achieve compromise, which all too often might be a rotten one, but would assume responsibility and uncompromisingly reach a decision alone. Roland Concin, the long-standing Head of Production, once observed accurately that Mateschitz stood by what he had said: "One word from him and a train could drive over it, but it would still stand firm."

When forming a careful opinion, expert knowledge and competence mattered more to him than rank and status. If necessary, he would also skip over the line of command. Each manager should be well-informed on the details or should bring with him the employee who knew them best. Mateschitz regarded it as a sign of strong leadership when an executive was not afraid of excellent employees, and was prepared to give them a job. He valued well-founded critical comments and would bear them in mind in his decision-making, and it was not surprising when he seemed unsurprised by such analyses, and after learning exactly what the situation was, would then act as he thought best. In his pursuit of a higher consideration which was not always immediately obvious, he would often be proved right.

However, if the situation changed fundamentally, or if he had new information, he was always ready to adopt a path that appeared even more promising. "What prevents me from being smarter today than yesterday," he would comment. "But we agreed that ...," might earn the riposte: "If you made a mistake yesterday, will you repeat it again today?". Dogmatic theoretical explanations were anathema to him: "That's the difference between Marx and a mess," meant in this context more or less that it might be good in theory, but was unsuitable in practice. As a quick and flexible thinker, he could not bear to listen to lengthy explanations of the obvious, and he wanted to remain in charge of the concern, "as long as the people leave it brighter than they were when they came."

Mateschitz saw his employees as under an obligation to draw on his expertise and experience. He expected his staff to ask him if they needed advice or help. That is not a matter of course and requires independent thinking, courage, flexibility, self-discipline, and character. For employees coming from companies in which rigid hierarchies, traditional career paths, precise processes, and clear systems severely limit the radius of operation of the individual, Red Bull may precipitate a culture shock, like the insecurity of the prisoner released into freedom.

But Mateschitz did not see it as a disgrace not to know something. However, his patience was likely to be severely tested by excuses and evasions, especially if they were an insult to his intelligence. Mateschitz made high demands of himself and his staff. He insisted on loyalty and professionalism. Professional, for him, meant knowing what your tasks were, making decisions, and acting upon them (instead of just talking), making a contribution and not expecting a free lunch. He saw employees who regarded the firm as a "feeding trough" as the very opposite of that.

At Red Bull, employees with ideas were granted plenty of scope and maximum design flexibility, and new staff members had the benefit of the doubt. Generous resources and budgets were made available in order to accomplish the tasks at hand, with the demand that they should be used in a businesslike manner and that employees should behave as if it were their own money. However, modesty and moderation at a personal level should never be confused with pettiness and cheese-paring in business. It is not always easy to find a balance between the two. It is very tempting to wrongly relate the attributes of the Red Bull brand to one's own person. The brand personality of Red Bull may be unpredictable and non-conformist, but this by no means implies that employees must or may behave that way themselves. The error in thinking like this becomes clear when we imagine an unpredictable financial management or a non-conformist legal department. The characteristics of the brand are not a competence profile for staff selection. And equally, generous investments in the brand must not be misunderstood by the staff as an invitation to personal craving for status and extravagance. The thing is always more important than the individual, and a healthy distance from ourselves enables us to recognize our limitations more easily. Mateschitz regarded it as a matter of importance, and repeatedly demanded of the Management and the Human Resources department, that they should ensure that people remained modest and did not become too full of themselves. If Mateschitz himself was asked about a success, he would often reply: "But we were only fooling around a bit."

What doubtless characterized the head of Red Bull more than anything else was his tireless interest in people and ideas. Every day he would be visited by athletes, artists, employees, customers, and business partners who would try to arouse his interest in one of their ideas. And if they were compatible with Red Bull, Mateschitz loved to enable these ideas to take wing. As a patient listener he was always in search of unusual and unconventional ideas and market opportunities. As such, he was always the driving force behind the innovation within the company. Irrespective of whether the ideas were large- or small-scale dreams, the main focus lay always on the individual and his role. Mateschitz was prepared to be filled with enthusiasm and to be inspired by these ideas, and he would frequently remove any obstacles if he was able to do so.

Mateschitz would take the time, however long was necessary, until the dream was told in full. The waiting times that inevitably resulted before an appointment to see him were legendary, because he could be so enthusiastic about an idea. His timetable was determined not by his appointments diary, but by the narrative. Tina Deutner, his assistant, who was present at virtually all meetings, frequently had to remind him gently that down below in Hangar 7—on hold, as it were, as on a crowded runway—other people were waiting to speak to him. When the discussion was over, he would often say: "Tina, who's next?"

At this point I should like to say a few words about myself, my career at Red Bull, and the appreciation I experienced within the company and from Dietrich Mateschitz. It was in late summer 1995, and I was preparing to take my law exams when I received a phone call from Frau Köstlinger from Salzburg. She had already contacted me once and offered me a job with the waste disposal department in Salzburg, which I had politely refused. At that time, at the beginning of my career, I still wanted above all to become a lawyer. She said that she now had the right job for me. We agreed on a meeting and she told me about Red Bull, the company's expansion, and that the global brand matters and upcoming product approvals were to be coordinated by a lawyer. Following my legal studies in Linz I had completed a postgraduate course of study in the United States and worked in the courts for three years as a lawyer. A career as a lawyer seemed inevitable, but I thought that spending some time gaining in-house experience in an international concern would not be a bad thing.

And so, during the next round of discussions a meeting was arranged with the corporate management. The next Monday saw me sitting at 8 a.m. opposite Dietrich Mateschitz in Fuschl am See. He was dressed casually and with a three-day beard, while I was somewhat inappropriately clad in suit and tie. After the conversation, Red Bull was no longer merely a possibility for me; I wanted the job at all costs. Further discussions with the head coaches and quarterbacks followed. The two head coaches Hans Peter Vriens and Norbert Kraihamer had joined Red Bull one year previously. Kraihamer had come from Salomon and was Mateschitz's right hand. He looked after France and the UK as well as all the coordination. Vriens had come from Procter & Gamble and was in charge of the remaining marketing and sales team. The quarterbacks Manfred Hückel, Markus Krebs, and Markus Pichler were offensive players and brand ambassadors, responsible for the expansion in the individual countries, at the time primarily with the help of distributors.

Vriens was in favor of a Spanish lawyer with German roots for the open position. At the time, the executives cast their votes by means of paperclips: three paperclips meant unreserved support for a candidate ("If he doesn't come I'm leaving"); two paperclips indicated agreement, and one paperclip stood for total rejection ("If he comes I'm leaving"). Nonetheless, I clearly managed to win the vote. Even Vriens must have awarded me two paperclips. He remained with the company until 1999. Mateschitz had justified doubts regarding the candidate from Spain. As it transpired during a short period of cooperation with him for the Spanish market just a few weeks later, he was proved right.

So at the time of publication (2023) I have been working for Red Bull for almost thirty years, and during this time, whenever I had a professional matter to discuss I could always be sure of the undivided attention of Dietrich Mateschitz. And on the rare occasions when I had a personal request, he would always offer me his support. The increased level of attention could be observed physically: his body would literally jerk, and his facial expression and attitude would switch immediately to active listening. An example was when my eldest daughter broke her collarbone for the third time and a complicated operation was necessary, my request to be allowed to consult the shoulder specialist Prof. Herbert Resch of the Private Medical University, which was supported by Red Bull, for advice was answered without hesitation: "But of course, Volker. That's what he's there for."

Of course there were also occasions during my time at Red Bull when I disappointed him. Those few occasions were never quickly forgiven and forgotten, but were like wounds which are slow to heal and whose scars are still visible years later. In any case, major breaches of trust cannot be forgiven as in a private relationship, but must be immediately and systematically penalized within a company for specific reasons and in the interests of prevention.

Of course, Mateschitz had faults and weaknesses too. He said of himself that "real implementation was never my strong point." In any case, he had his Board of Directors for that, and his departmental heads and project leaders, whose "character and competence were beyond question." To Walter Bachinger he once commented, roguishly and confidentially: "You must not believe all I say," by which he meant that in the heat of the moment he might sometimes be persuaded to say something which he would then expect us to examine in greater detail. Moreover, he was seldom prepared to agree to a compromise and he was not always punctual. As an individual he was wont to build up an aura around himself, as he had previously done with the brand. I think the outside world should not pass judgment on him for that. Let he who is without fault cast the first stone. And then, our weaknesses are often our greatest strengths. Focused on arriving at a consensus, decisive and always focused on the task in hand, Mateschitz was not free of fault on a personal level, but was an entrepreneurial institution.

There cannot be a successor for him in the narrow sense. As in other world-class concerns, at whose head there is not only a truly charismatic visionary but also a brilliant founder and innovator—I am thinking, for example, of Steve Jobs at Apple—similarly, in the case of Red Bull it is impossible to imagine a one-to-one replacement for the cosmopolitan, tradition-conscious individualist Dietrich Mateschitz. Earlier on, when I was asked about succession plans for a time after Mateschitz, I always answered: Let us hope that he will continue to head the company for a long time. We shall have to see what will come after him. Now, after his death, my answer is: We shall endeavor to continue to run Red Bull as he would have wished for as long as possible. This aim is also supported unreservedly by the shareholders, for which we are thankful and appreciative.

Dietrich Mateschitz the institution was the determining factor which from the beginning made Red Bull into a concern that was run with a sense of purpose and with a clear set of values, so that it continues to be so today. A company that values people not only as a production factor but sees them in the sense of Viktor Frankl as a source of creativity and innovation.

To enable people and their ideas to take flight exercises an almost infectious appeal for all those who want to realize their ideas and who see a partner in Red Bull. In this way, the concern has become a home of excellence. The numerous top performers among the Red Bull athletes, artists, employees, and partners all share one thing in common; they have willingly and independently taken on a huge task, have worked diligently to strengthen their talents, and in this task have found their purpose in life within Frankl's meaning of the phrase. The implementation of this fundamental thought, the triad of esteem, innovation, and success, is only possible within an attractive concern, in which ultimately the individual forms the focus of attention. Red Bull has confidence in them and trusts them to fulfill their specific, self-chosen, and individual tasks.

Back then, in that job interview, I could not imagine the lasting effect that Dietrich Mateschitz and Red Bull would have on me. Today, thirty years later, I am thankful for the opportunities he offered me. To be able to carry out at Red Bull that job which best corresponds to my interests and abilities. Today I know that I would not have been as happy in a career as a lawyer and I would not have been able to make use of my potential to the full. At the end Mateschitz also supported me in my own entrepreneurial ambitions in the real-estate redeployment deaurea. When I presented to him a concept financed through the bank, he simply said that he liked the idea and I would not need a bank. Without more ado, he agreed to finance my project. But ultimately I am most grateful to Dietrich Mateschitz because he appreciated my work, and trusted me and the work of my colleagues in the two departments, Human Resources and Legal Affairs.

4 PARADOXICAL INTENTION

" I don't have to put up with everything I do."
VIKTOR FRANKL

Our survival as a species has always been ensured by a healthy portion of fear. In general, it was the fearful individuals who tended to survive, while the (over-) confident and (hyper-) aggressive ones died out through natural selection or elimination by the other members of their tribe. A healthy portion of fear makes us alert. In the early centuries of human existence, not being watchful for a moment could be just as deadly as non-ritualized aggression which deviated from the norm. In the first case, the saber-toothed tiger would pounce, and in the second, the fellow members of the tribe would make short work of you. Fear is our constant companion, and fears were passed on from generation to generation across millions of years of our evolutionary history. Primeval fears like those of snakes or spiders are not learned, but handed down. Anxiety disorders can be inherited or caused by traumatic experiences during childhood. A panic attack means complete loss of control, the ability to interact with one's surroundings is lost, and the individual is thrown back on himself and his primal fears. In order to be able to lead a normal and autonomous life, we must control our fears, and in order to perform heroic deeds, we must overcome them.

The mountaineer and alpinist Viktor Frankl suffered from vertigo. For this reason, he had to overcome this fear from an early age in order to be able to lead a meaningful life. In his youth, when his friend took him for the first time to climb on the Mizzi-Langer Wall in the Vienna Woods, he realized how frightened he was. When he stood at the top of the 873-feet-high cliff, his knees gave way and he had to force himself to look down. From then onward, Frankl repeatedly forced himself to go into the mountains and to overcome his fear. Quite intuitively, he anticipated decades of psychotherapeutic intervention in anxiety disorders by repeatedly facing the situation which triggered the fear. When he was later asked what had prompted him to go climbing, he said: "To be frank, my fear of it."

Frankl went even further. He demanded of his patients that they should wish for the very thing they were frightened of, in such an exaggerated form that it became ludicrous. He would demand of students who were very nervous and who arrived at the consultation in a state of alarm, that they should make themselves even more nervous. The patients tried it, but Frankl was not so easy to satisfy. "Even more nervous," he demanded. Then they would start to laugh, and their nervousness was gone. He asked patients suffering from agoraphobia to imagine that they would fall down dead if they were to go out into the street, just as all others who had dared to do the same thing before them had also dropped down dead. Other patients were to imagine that they would suffocate immediately if they were to use a lift which then got stuck. "Paradoxical intention" means to face the frightening situation and to exaggerate it until it becomes laughable. In this way we become stronger than our fear; we learn to overcome it and we are no longer helplessly at its mercy.

To keep death in mind does not only mean an exaggeration, but like Don Juan Matus we can also call on it for advice. To carry out actions with the awareness of one's own mortality gives them a whole new significance. In our awareness of finality and irrevocability, all decisions, be they important or trivial, large or small, must be made carefully. "People usually see only the stubble field of transience; what they fail to see are the full barns of the past. In this past, nothing is irrevocably lost; rather, it is all unlosably preserved," observed Frankl.

The more we are aware of our insignificance in the course of time, the greater the importance of the sum total of all our decisions will become for our lives. Viktor Frankl wrote: "He who has done his duty all things considered, does not fear death. Only those who have lived wrongly see erroneously in death the just punishment which we cannot escape. We should live in such a way that we can be friends with death while still on Earth." He clearly sees death as part of life. Frankl rejects an explicit link with extreme sport, even though in extreme mountaineering, situations between being and not being are by no means unusual. Frankl did not go into the mountains to lead "a life provoked by death" (Gottfried Benn), or to be better than others. "Alpinists compete with and see only one person as a rival, namely themselves. They demand something of themselves, possibly an achievement, but also a renunciation," he wrote in *Bergerlebnis und Sinnerfahrung*.

For Frankl, the overcoming of his vertigo was an exercise in honing the "contrary strength of the mind," and climbing his "life peak," the Rax, became the elixir of life: "Must I always accept everything I do? Can I not be stronger than my fear? That was what I asked myself, I, who was frightened of climbing: Who is stronger: I or my weaker self? I can defy it. There is something in people ... the contrary spirit against the fears and weaknesses of the mind." In order to arrive at the limits of the possible, we must practice renunciation, expose ourselves to stress, health-preserving stress, or if necessary also the stress which makes us ill. We must practice renunciation and we must overcome fears and weaknesses.

"In contrast to the individual who lives, biologically speaking, in a gentle cycle, the climber in the mountains does not choose the 'path of least resistance', but prefers to seek out for his climbing tour the most difficult route he is just able to manage." In life, as in climbing, the rule is to fathom out the marginal conditions of what is only just possible. "And lo and behold: he will find that it is like the horizon: with every step that he takes towards it, the horizon recedes in front of him; as he approaches it, he pushes it further away—exactly as, for example in the history of 'extreme' and 'free' climbing, the boundary of what is humanly possible is pushed ever further away. By pushing this boundary ever further away, he will also surpass himself ..."

How Red Bull sounds out boundaries and surpasses itself

// Not bad for a beverage company! //
LEWIS HAMILTON

For Viktor Frankl, sport in general played a not insignificant role within the value principles of meaningfulness and purposefulness in life, but also within the method of the paradoxical intention. Red Bull, too, has always had close links with sport, and within precisely the same meaning as in Frankl's philosophy it also has a dual explanation. Of course, on the one hand it is a question of overcoming fears and sounding out limits. But on the other it is always a question of finding a way out of the "mediocrity trap" and giving a sense of purpose to one's actions.

The marketing of Red Bull set new standards from an early stage. After all, an innovative product first had to be introduced and advertised. "Brand love," identification with the brand, was at least as important as "can love," the appreciation of the can. If the effect is the foundation for the resounding success of the drink Red Bull, then the creation of the content marketing for the brand is the cathedral built on that foundation.

The breakthrough came quite literally overnight. Formula One pilot Gerhard Berger was the first Red Bull motor sports athlete. When Mateschitz asked him what it would cost for him to sponsor a drinking scene, Berger replied in his frank Tyrolean manner: "More than you can afford, Didi." In 1989, after a season that had been difficult from a sporting point of view, and in which Berger had frequently had to retire from the race because of technical problems with his Ferrari and had also been injured in Imola, towards the end of the season he won the Portuguese Grand Prix. After the victory he was filmed from a distance against the sunset, drinking a can of Red Bull. The next day, Red Bull was sold out everywhere in Austria. From that day onward, Berger and Mateschitz were close friends as well as joint owners of a logistics company.

Mateschitz and his friend Chalerm Yoovidhya were both fans of motor sport, and Formula One had always radiated a particular fascination. Even before the founding of Red Bull, when Mateschitz was still working for Blendax and the later shareholder and partner Chalerm T. C. Pharmaceuticals Co. Ltd. was the sales representative of Blendax in Thailand, the two of them dreamed of one day being able to afford a Formula One team, as sponsors or perhaps even as owners.

The drinking scene in Portugal and its resounding success strengthened Mateschitz in his belief that Formula One was the right marketing platform for Red Bull. It generated the greatest advertising pressure worldwide, and no other event reached comparable gross coverage within the target group potential that was of particular interest for energy drinks. Measured by contacts within the target group, there was no more effective form of advertising than sponsoring the premier class of motor sport.

Six years and the sale of countless millions of cans later, the dream came true: Red Bull was able to afford to purchase a majority share and take on the main sponsoring at Sauber Motorsport. In the next ten years the international roll out of the brand was supported by the Formula One involvement at Sauber, and from 2001 also by the Arrows team. Red Bull had a strong partner in Sauber, but wanted to achieve more than the midfield positions. Moreover, they had no influence on the operations of the Sauber team. And so, from 2002, they negotiated an entry into Tom Walkinshaw's Arrows team. The failure of the negotiations meant the ultimate failure of the Arrows. In 2004, following four years in Formula One without success, Ford decided to sell not only the Cosworth engine factory in Northampton, but also the Jaguar racing team in Milton Keynes. The negotiations for the takeover took place under great time pressure because Ford was also considering the immediate closure of the works. Ultimately, the takeover of the team including the factory in Milton Keynes represented a win-win situation for both Ford and Red Bull. Ford was able to avoid the costs of closing down, amounting to a figure in the double-figure millions; and Red Bull acquired a fully-fledged Formula One team including a construction firm, and without incalculable debts, as would have been the case with the Arrows.

Mateschitz was aware from the beginning that it was not the purchase price, but making up the investment deficit and the continuous financing costs for the team and the factory that would be the deciding factor if his aim was to compete in the world championship. In this context, he was wont to say, "The least expensive part in Formula One is purchasing the team." This applied all the more because Red Bull was not a manufacturing team; they did not manufacture the motors, and so were not able to allocate the developments to the general automobile production.

After the takeover, Mateschitz invested systematically in staff and technology. Helmut Marko, respectfully known as "the Doctor" and responsible for the motor sport (Marko has a doctorate in law), brought in Christian Horner, whom he already knew from his Formula 3000 time, to head the team. A year later, Adrian Newey also joined the team as motor sport engineer. As "design guru" he was responsible in 2010 for enabling Red Bull Racing to bring home the first of a total of five construction world championships to date.*

In order to provide young drivers with suitable training opportunities, from 2006 the Minardi team "Scuderia Toro Rosso", now "Alpha Tauri", was created as a novices team in Faenza. Before he was signed by Red Bull Racing in 2009, Sebastian Vettel, who had been supported by Red Bull since his kart racing days, was able to perfect his outstanding talent in the cockpit of Toro Rosso. Vettel won four world championships with Red Bull Racing from 2010. That forced even Lewis Hamilton to admit that it was, "Not bad for a beverage company." Mateschitz had every right to be proud of the achievements of his teams.

When we speak of Red Bull and sport, we cannot possibly ignore soccer. Like the two Formula One teams Red Bull Racing and Scuderia Alpha Tauri, most soccer clubs also represent shareholdings and are thus investments which Red Bull frequently makes in order to better control and develop projects.

The Red Bull Academy in Salzburg-Liefering forms part of the soccer endeavor RB Salzburg. Located in the east of Salzburg, at the confluence of the Salzach and the Saalach, at the so-called Saalachspitz, there is an extensive continuous riparian zone where you can find morel mushrooms in spring.

---

* His life and especially his time at Red Bull are impressively described in his autobiography, published in 2018 with the title *How to Build a Car*.

The secret as to where exactly they are to be found is passed on from generation to generation and is more carefully kept than the—admittedly somewhat tattered of late—Swiss banking secrecy. From the mid-1960s this was also the site of the Salzburg trotting track, after the course at the location in Rennbahnstraße in Parsch had been swallowed up by the city's expansion. Where formerly the horses in harness trotted round, since 2014 the 32-acre space has housed the Red Bull Academy for soccer and ice hockey, with seven soccer pitches, two ice rinks, a multi-function hall, a motorikpark, a bodybuilding gym, an athletics space, a wellness area, and a boarding school. The Academy offers 200 soccer and 200 ice hockey talents training opportunities at the highest level. In addition to the youth teams, FC Liefering also trains at the site.

Before the construction began there were discussions as to whether it made sense to invest millions in an academy to train young talents. The association lays down fairly rigid regulations governing the training of young players for the teams, especially relating to the change of residence and the contractual engagement of young people. One might therefore be of the opinion that the money would be better invested in scouting and headhunting talented players from other clubs, and in paying higher salaries. At the end of the discussion, during which both the legal and the financial departments believed they must fulfill their duty to warn and protect, Mateschitz nonetheless decided to build the Academy, saying that this was not only a financial matter, but that it was a question of promoting talent in the long term. Today the Academy makes sense, not only as regards the promotion of talent, but also economically.

The success of FC and EC Red Bull Salzburg, and also that of RB Leipzig, is due a considerable extent to the young players from the Academy, who set out year after year to prove themselves in the competitive teams. The training concept is consistent. The playing philosophy is internalized in the youth teams. The training for the ice hockey Rookies, with their motto *Speed and Skill*, is many times harder than that of the soccer players. Let us hope that the latter will follow the example of the former. Much emphasis is laid on school-based education; in top-class sport, both mind and body are necessary. And so at the Academy, the division of time is "51 percent school, 49 percent sport".

FC Liefering plays a particular role in the soccer training concept. It participates in the second-highest Austrian division and thus forms the link between the Academy teams and the adult teams. Here the U 18 and U 19 talents learn to assert themselves against adult players at an early stage. In 2008, when the national soccer league excluded the amateur teams of Red Bull Salzburg and Austria Wien from the competition because there was to be a reduction from twelve to ten teams, Mateschitz immediately ordered them to create another farm team in the second division of the adult sport. This did not succeed until 2012 with the rise of FC Liefering, which had developed from USK Anif.

The teams play an attractive pressing, which can only be executed to perfection with young, ambitious players. Since "Professor" Ralf Rangnick instilled this soccer philosophy consistently, Red Bull makes its teams not only take wings, but also one title after another. Their orders are to dominate at home and surprise internationally. In the meantime,

RB Leipzig has also established its position in one of the top places of the German soccer league, and won the DFB Cup in 2022 and 2023 consecutively.

For a long time, soccer at Red Bull was seen as being unattractive and not consistent with the brand because of the protagonists and the environment. Mateschitz even commented that he wanted to be incapacitated if he started to champion the masses in this game. It was hardly surprising in view of the violent and radicalized hooligans, who prevented fans and sports-loving children and families from attending stadiums, not to mention the officials who were more interested in self-presentation than in the sport itself, and the player transfers and players' salaries financed from illicit earnings. Corruption in the clubs hit the headlines regularly. So it was not far-fetched to regard soccer as not exactly being a popular representative of the Red Bull brand. Accordingly, many people were surprised when soccer was made socially acceptable overnight for Red Bull. Many staff members were very surprised when Austria Salzburg, which was teetering on the edge of bankruptcy, became Red Bull Salzburg.

The occasion for this investment was the sorry state of Salzburg Austria in the mid-2000s. Following its sporting successes in the 1990s, the club had overextended itself financially, and in 2005 it was threatened with relegation and bankruptcy. The President of the club, Rudolf Quehenberger, had asked Mateschitz more than once whether Red Bull might be prepared to invest as main sponsor, but Mateschitz had politely refused every time. In 2005, when the situation had become dramatic because of the club's over-indebtedness, Red Bull assumed responsibility and repositioned the club on a new, sound basis through its sponsoring. That meant that Salzburg was spared developments like those experienced by fans, officials, and politicians in Innsbruck, Graz, and Klagenfurt, not to mention a highly subsidized and temporarily abandoned EM stadium in Carinthia: art projects have been realized there, and trees have been grown on the pitch.

The investment in Salzburg was made for a specific reason, but it was fundamental. In the first years, the sponsoring of soccer as a mass sport alongside Formula One was financially difficult to manage, and the athletes in the extreme sports provided better image pictures for the concern. But in 2005 Red Bull had developed from a niche product to become the third-largest drinks producer worldwide. In Austria, more energy drinks were being sold than cans of cola. What was decisive, however, was that an analysis of European and international soccer indicated that Red Bull could also be correctly positioned in the soccer environment. Soccer clubs and players act increasingly strategically and follow a playing philosophy. Trainers like Pep Guardiola, Ralf Rangnick, Jürgen Klopp, and Thomas Tuchel, as well as players like Lionel Messi, Neymar, and Leroy Sané set new standards not only in sport, but also intellectually. Soccer clubs like Manchester City, Barcelona, and Bayern München had risen to become global brands. The earnings from television fees, merchandising, and sponsoring were invested in players and infrastructure, from which ultimately the soccer fan also profited. And so a visit to a stadium became exciting not only for committed soccer fans, but also for a broader spectrum of sports lovers, and could also become a family event. The prerequisite for this is that there must be a clear boundary set to the violent hooligan scene. If this approach was to be followed, new scope for design could be opened up, which would also make soccer of interest for Red Bull. Or, as Mateschitz said: "But now the time was ripe to make soccer too."

There were intensive discussions as to whether Red Bull should also become involved in one of the major leagues. The Austrian soccer league had the advantage that because of the league structure, each year there was a very good chance that the team might qualify to compete in the Champions League and the Europa League and hence that there would be an opportunity for an international surprise. Nonetheless, there was a good deal of patriotism involved in the investment in Red Bull Salzburg.

Austria still lacks the necessary preconditions to be able to compete permanently for the trophies in international competitions. Good players do not remain in their home league. Their careers are often short, and they want to move as soon as possible to the major clubs in Germany, England, or Spain. The Austrian League is a training league with an annual income from television advertising of approximately € 30 million. After the costs and shares in the costs have been subtracted, this results in a payment of up to € 3 million per year for each club. Only a few clubs survive the qualifying rounds for international championships, which is their reward for reaching the top places in the league. By comparison, the German soccer league has advertising revenues of € 1 billion, and the Premier League even more. There a leading club will earn hundreds of millions of euros from television fees. An analysis of the eighty clubs in the four English leagues (including the Premier League, founded in 1992) within forty years of professional soccer shows that, in the long term, the amount of players' salaries is the sole factor that determines the sporting success of a club. The stars at Manchester United, Real Madrid, Barca, and Bayern München earn € 500,000, per week, nota bene. Top clubs pay no less than € 300 million in salaries to their players. That means that some fifty percent of the total budget of a club is reserved for the players' salaries. If a club has long-term ambitions to win the Champions League trophy, it will therefore need an annual budget of over € 500 million. Accordingly, only clubs with high revenues from television fees, spectators, and sponsoring will be able to participate at the top of the international business.

This development was intensified by the verdict by the European Court of Justice in the Bosman case in 1995. The judgment determined that at the end of the term of their contract, players could change to another club on a free transfer, and also that there would be no restrictions on foreign players in the squad. As a result, the special provisions of the national leagues were invalid. It was no coincidence that Ajax Amsterdam last won the Champions League in 1995 in Vienna under Louis van Gaal.

Ralf Rangnick, who worked for the soccer division at Red Bull in various positions between 2012–2021, was passionately enthusiastic about bringing the best soccer talents to Red Bull, where they could be promoted optimally and their individual strengths developed. As a result, the Red Bull teams were increasingly on an equal footing with the best clubs in the world, and he repeatedly argued in favor of purchasing a club in England. With three times the advertising revenues of the German soccer league, the Premier League really would be great fun. And from a German point of view, the soccer they play there is certainly capable of improvement—a paradise for Rangnick, Klopp and Tuchel as "aid workers".

The takeover of an English club with a long tradition in nouveau-riche style did not suit the taste of Dietrich Mateschitz, however. The die had already been cast and a decision had been taken in favor of Leipzig, in spite of the 50+1 rule which, unlike the situation in England, does not permit the takeover of a club as a joint-stock company. Mateschitz had had a "trial run" in Leipzig, had visited the regions, the city, and the stadium, and had then decided that Leipzig and Red Bull could be a good match for each other. As a region, Saxony had long been without a team in the top league. The project RB Leipzig ought to be greeted with enthusiasm. There was only a minor flaw in the argument: there was no club to take over. There was no soccer club anywhere in sight, not in the first league, not in the second or the third league, and not even in the regional league. Andreas Sadlo, the sports agent from Fuschl am See, found what he was looking for in the fifth class of Oberliga Nordost. For the 2009/10 season, RB Leipzig took over the starting rights of SSV Markranstädt.

With much blood, sweat, and tears the club was raised into the top league, where it arrived seven years later in the 2016/17 season. The project was not a takeover, but a decision to form and anchor a club in the region. The fans appreciated this long-term commitment and the associated responsibility, and correspondingly identified themselves with the club, even though it had only a small number of full members who therefore had a vote.

The clubs in New York and São Paulo round out the global soccer commitment of Red Bull. Soccer is the most popular sport in the United States up to high school. It seems very likely that in the next few years, soccer will catch up with the "Big 4": American football, baseball, basketball, and ice hockey. And Brazil is a soccer-mad nation, so from a marketing point of view, it made sense to establish a club in the first league for a relatively small sum of money.

Apart from the revenues from the energy drink, sporting successes, television fees, income from spectators, and transfer fees, Mateschitz's real interest lay in the soccer academies. Not only in Salzburg, but also in Leipzig, São Paulo, and New York. The young players are not only promoted on the sports field, but also receive in most cases a humanist education. Both aspects justify the investment in the academies. For Mateschitz, the prime focus lay in the meaningful aspect of football as a sport for young people.

The soccer project is a prime example of the forward-looking analysis and situational policy within the concern. And if this commitment on behalf of young people turns out to be a deciding factor for the sporting success of the teams, then of course the pleasure is all the greater: thus nothing less than the vision of a global network of synergies is fulfilled, something which has hitherto not existed in the field of soccer.

But let us leave soccer and return once more to the beginning. Particularly in its early years, Red Bull was known for its sponsoring of extreme sports, in which fears should be overcome and limits tested in the sense of Viktor Frankl's paradoxical intention. The protagonists were hand-picked; the sportspeople were to represent the Red Bull brand. It was not sufficient to be one of the best in a particular sport; there also had to be a fit between the character of the athlete and Red Bull. Few sportspeople embodied this symbiosis as well as Robby Naish. Mr. Windsurfing embodied the world of Red Bull perhaps better than any other. With his sail no. US-1111, the pioneer of windsurfing became world champion a total of twenty-four times. He achieved this for the first time in 1976; at the age of thirteen he was the youngest world champion in history. In 2001, he set a new speed record in kitesurfing off Gran Canaria with a speed of 70.37 kph (38.4 knots). At the time of writing (2023), at the age of sixty, he stands on his surfboard almost every day; for him it is "almost as if you can walk on water. It is an incredible freedom."

Anyone who has heard him giving one of his lectures understands why Naish is the perfect brand ambassador. He stands in front of his audience and speaks freely while slides showing scenes from his life run in the background: Naish as a child in Kailua on the island of O'ahu in Hawaii, where he grew up; with his wife and children; with his sports cars. And of course all sorts of photos of surfing: windsurfing, kitesurfing, foil surfing, and stand-up paddling; Naish on crutches after a kitesurfing accident that broke his pelvis in the summer of 2016; an X-ray showing the screws in his pelvis; and Naish at the Aloha Classics—five months later, in November 2016!

Since 1979, Robby Naish has also been an entrepreneur. His firms are involved in the development of surfing gear, and he makes use of his passion to market better products. His innovations include the development of shorter surfboards, the viewing panel in the sail, the foot strap, and the trapeze. Naish goes surfing almost every day, because that is also the "prerequisite for developing good products." If someone suggests to him that it does not sound much like working in an office and wonders what his employees would say to it, Naish replies: "You mustn't imagine Naish as a typical company. We aren't an insurance firm, but we develop and sell toys for the finest thing in the world. I don't have a desk of my own, let alone my own office. When I'm in the office I sit down anywhere where there is a space. And if necessary, if one of my employees needs the desk, I just move. It works well. In the Naish office people are always coming and going. We have no hierarchies like those in other companies. We're a mixed bunch from all over the world, including a lot of Europeans. Everyone knows what he has to do and he is free to do it as and when he thinks fit. And some of that work takes place not at a desk, but on or by the water." Mateschitz thought up his own firm in exactly the same way in the early 1980s, and that is also how he ran it during the early years.

Robby Naish's links with Red Bull go back to the early 1990s. On the occasion of the annual business plan meeting in Kitzbühel, people spent many days talking about sales plans. And that it was essential to get out, take on the competition and win the contest on the shelves, one can at a time. When, at the end, Naish gave his lecture it was a reminder of the company's roots, of the reason why Mateschitz had founded the company. Red Bull was not founded to keep competitors in check, but to make people and ideas take wing—for employees in search of a grand task, for sportspeople who love a challenge, and for artists who create something unique. But above all for young people, whom Naish and Mateschitz wanted to encourage to follow their dreams. "Sport can change the world. It gives hope, motivation, self-confidence, friendship, and a purpose in life. Watersports are particularly powerful. To be out there in nature, to glide across the water, to make use of the wind or the waves, and to use the power of water as your motor, is fun and enriches your life. So grab a board—and head outdoors! And I also encourage kids to 'pull the plug'. Nowadays they spend far too much time with their computer and their cellphone." We remember: Frankl, too, saw in sport the modern form of asceticism.

Naish concluded his lecture in Kitzbühel with an anecdote. He had met Mateschitz for the first time in the late 1990s. They understood each other immediately. After it became clear that they both loved fast cars, Naish was invited by Mateschitz to a drive in his Ferrari GTO. Mateschitz drove up a mountain road as far as the pass. There he got out and asked Naish to drive back down. Naish, knowing what the Ferrari was worth, thanked him politely but declined, saying that he could not afford to write off a car like that. Mateschitz then gave him the choice: Either Naish drove or he walked back home. Mateschitz's son Mark had been listening to the lecture. He added that to that day he had not been allowed to drive the Ferrari ...

Berger and Naish were followed by numerous other athletes, whose career ran alongside Red Bull for a while. The list is endless. Aksel Lund Svindal can stand here as a representative of all the rest. For sixteen years, he was one of the great ski racers in the Ski World Championship circus. He won the Alpine Ski World Cup in four out of five disciplines, recorded thirty-six victories in 386 World Cup races, and became the Olympic champion twice and the World Champion five times. He was someone who never simulated but always remained authentic. Not a dreamer, but a realist. And above all, someone who never gave up despite countless setbacks through severe injuries, and who always fought back. In fact, Svindal—like Frankl—fights primarily against himself and not against his rivals.

Felix Baumgartner was someone who tested his limits and surpassed them in a truly remarkable way. From 1997 he lived his Base-jump dreams with Red Bull. Baumgartner repeatedly polarized with his political predictions and statements, swimming against the tide and refusing to subordinate himself. He served in the army as a parachuting instructor at the Army Sports and Close-Quarters Combat Training School in Wiener Neustadt. There he was not prepared to follow "stupid orders", and was therefore decommissioned as "unsuitable for the army." In 1999, disguised as an office worker, he smuggled his parachute in his briefcase to the top of the Petronas Twin Towers in Kuala Lumpur and jumped from the 88th floor. In December 1999, he parachuted at 7 a.m. from the giant statue of Cristo Redentor on the Corcovado in Rio de Janeiro. The previous evening he had allowed himself to be locked in on the site. He climbed up the statue with the aid of a rope he had shot over the statue using a crossbow. The action took place with the active support of Red Bull employees, who whisked him by car to safety from the rapidly approaching police after the jump. The photos were seen all around the world. In 2003, Baumgartner was the first person to glide across the English Channel from Dover to Calais in his *Wingsuit SkyRay*. The flying machine had been developed with the support of Red Bull, and is used to this day under the name *Gryphon* as a military weapons system for surprise attacks by paratroopers. With the *Wingsuit* it is possible to carry out attacks rapidly and unnoticed at a distance of up to forty kilometers. Numerous other projects followed, always meticulously planned and with an outcome that would do credit to a James Bond film. All the same, one or the other Base Jump also ended in a brief spell in prison, including the jump in 2004 from the

Puente de las Américas bridge in Panama linking North and South America.

Baumgartner achieved his lighthouse project in 2012 with the Stratos Project. This required years of preparation and the overcoming of mental obstacles and legal impediments; he suffered from claustrophobia in a space suit, like Berger and Newey in the Formula One. For the Stratos Project, he jumped out of the stratosphere and set several world records: in short, it was the longest, highest, and fastest flight in the history of humankind. Countless safety measures had been implemented to save Baumgartner's life if he ended up in a flat spin with high G-forces, which would have made him lose consciousness. Red Bull helped Baumgartner to realize his dream, in line with the company vision, "to inspire people to dare great things." The costs of the project amounted to €25 million. The advertising value of Stratos was estimated at €1 billion. Two hundred television stations and networks reported on the event live. Eight million viewers followed it simultaneously in livestream on YouTube. That was a world record, which beat Barack Obama's inauguration, with seven million viewers, for top place. After that leap, Baumgartner ended his active career and moved to Switzerland.

Heinz Kinigadner was another exceptional talent and one of Mateschitz's few friends. Kinigadner is a motorcross legend. He won the World Championship in 1984 and 1985 in the 250-cc class on KTM. In the 1990s, he drove and won in motorcycle rallies. He won the Pharaohs Rally in 1994, the Paris–Peking Rally in 1995, and the Atlas Rally in 1996. He was Sports Manager at KTM from 1997. In early 2000, Mateschitz and he drove in the Paris–Dakar rally, during which Mateschitz injured his shoulder, making an operation in Innsbruck necessary. The friendship between the two men was strengthened by the accident.

At the end of July 2003, Kinigadner was struck by a great misfortune which changed his life. Kinigadner was attending the MotoGP at Sachsenring in Germany when he received a phone call: His son Hannes had suffered critical injuries during a charity rally for disabled children in Upper Austria. Mateschitz stepped in and had him brought to Salzburg to the intensive-care unit for accident surgery led by Prof. Herbert Resch. There the nineteen-year-old accident victim survived two cardiac arrests, a cerebellar infarction, and was saved from suffocation.

"Hannes had also injured his fifth cervical vertebra and his spinal cord in the accident. Once his condition was stable, it became clear that he was paralyzed from the neck downwards," said Kinigadner in a joint interview. The journalist wanted to know what the father's first thoughts were after he heard the diagnosis. Kinigadner thought for a moment. "I was very afraid. And yet my family and I were still hopeful." As a quadriplegic, Hannes has only limited movement in his arms. "That means I need help getting dressed, as well as eating, drinking, and washing. In fact, I need help with everything." The reporter asked what that meant for him. "It's difficult. But my family is very supportive and somehow you get used to it. You have to keep going."—"In that respect, Hannes is a role model for us all," said his father. "When we are tempted to fall into a depression, he's a tower of strength. No healthy person can imagine what it means to be a paraplegic. And although my brother is also confined to a wheelchair, I had absolutely no idea of the implications of this injury for one's daily life."

A year later the friends Dietrich Mateschitz and Heinz Kinigadner established the private foundation Wings for Life to support research into finding a cure for paraplegia. The *Wings for Life World Run* has been held since 2014, with the motto: "Run for those who can't walk." One hundred percent of the revenues of the Wings for Life Foundation are channeled into research into spinal injuries. In view of the fact that damaged nerve cells in the spinal cord are capable of regeneration following certain forms of treatment, we are justified in hoping that it may become possible to cure traumatic paraplegia.

And so there was a haunting scene when Kinigadner and Hannes attended the opening of Travel Birds, the travel agency of Marion Feichtner, the life partner of Mateschitz. Hannes was sitting at one of the tables and was giving an interview. He looked fit. "The nerves in the spinal cord are capable of regeneration. The problem of paraplegia is the subject of continuous research and we are beginning to understand it better. Now people are working on a solution. Serious research takes time, but I am quite sure that one day I shall be able to stand up out of this chair," he said with conviction and looked across to his father Heinz, who nodded in agreement.

Not everyone who lives an unusual life governed by extreme sport will die a natural death. A number of friends of Red Bull were killed in fatal accidents, during Red Bull events or outside a promotional event while practicing the hobby which was their passion. Ueli Gegenschatz, for example. He was a pioneer of the Swiss extreme sports scene and from 1995 was a member of the Red Bull Acro Team together with Hannes Arch—who also died in an accident in 2016—and Andreas Hediger. Within the framework of events sponsored by Red Bull, in 2009 Gegenschatz was caught by a sudden gust of wind while leaping from the Sunrise Tower in Zurich, lost control, and plunged to the ground. Two days later he died of the fatal injuries he sustained. The media spoke of the dark side of Red Bull, and that Red Bull drove people to their death for advertising purposes. After the death of Gegenschatz, his mother commented in an interview that he had always prepared "seriously and carefully and had always demonstrated his love of life in his jumps." She did not reproach Red Bull and did not believe that the company's marketing concept was to blame. That there is no substance in the allegations is evident to anyone who knows how the media function and who have any knowledge at all of Red Bull.

Red Bull gives people wings—and challenges everyone who sees life as the opposite of the daily grind, lethargy, and hopelessness, to realize their dreams and their goals. There is always an alternative: now and tomorrow we can decide which path we shall take. But for that we need to take full responsibility for our actions. Our life results from the sum of these actions. And those who recognize and are aware that their actions are final and irreversible, will decide carefully and always give of their best. Those who share this attitude see the world not as a burden but as a challenge which requires us to be active, and to seize the opportunities instead of complaining and blaming others for the standstill and boredom. Red Bull encourages us to go our way in freedom and with a sense of personal responsibility, with an clear mind and open eyes. Red Bull is more than just the consumption of a can of energy drink;

Red Bull is an attitude to life—the attitude of a warrior like the one described in Carlos Castaneda's *The Teachings of Don Juan*.

This attitude to life coincides with that practiced by Dietrich Mateschitz. It becomes the guide for all the marketing activities of Red Bull. Red Bull adopted a new approach and became the epitome of innovative marketing. Red Bull implemented one project after another beyond the mainstream—polarizing, perfectionist, witty, and often with a hint of self-irony.

Nothing embodies freedom more graphically than flying. Flying is the dream of humankind. In 1992, the first Red Bull Flight Day was held in Vienna. The participants hurled themselves from a ramp into the water below in their self-made flying machines. The dream of humankind came true for a few seconds, or sometimes even for minutes. A jury assessed not only the distance flown but also the originality of the flying machine. The spectacle is usually followed by hundreds of thousands of viewers on site and on television. To this day, flight days are held in more than fifty cities worldwide.

The Flight Days are often accompanied by the Flying Bulls, whose fleet consists of immaculately maintained and restored historic aircraft. The Flying Bulls have at their disposal a fleet of the finest and rarest aircraft in history. The history of the Flying Bulls began during the 1980s. Sigi Angerer, a pilot with Tyrolean Airways, had a weakness for historic aircraft and collected Warbirds, which he had brought to Innsbruck and restored there. The purchase of a legendary Chance Vought F4U-4 Corsair brought Angerer and Dietrich Mateschitz together. The idea of the Flying

Bulls was born and the fleet then grew with the worldwide success of the energy drinks. The aircraft eventually found a home in Hangar 7 and 8 at Salzburg Airport. The Flying Bulls aircraft are a popular attraction at the Flight Day and at other Red Bull events and air shows.

Sigi Angerer and Dietrich Mateschitz were also friends. When Mateschitz invited a guest to a "flightseeing" session, he and Sigi would take their seats in the cockpit at the front and the passengers would enjoy the views of the mountains from the back seats. Occasionally one of these scenic flights would take in a valley in the northern Alps that appeared to end in a vertical mountain wall. The passengers had radio contact with the pilots. As they flew low along the valley, Mateschitz would calmly say to Sigi: "Don't you think we ought to think about pulling the plane up?" No answer from Sigi. Mateschitz would repeat the request. The approaching rock wall would have the full attention of the passengers. Sigi Angerer would then say, equally calmly: "I can't get its nose up." Silence. Seconds, which feel like minutes, and everyone's face would suddenly pale. Upon reaching what looked as if it must be the head of the valley, suddenly the valley walls opened up to the east and the machine banked steeply to follow the curve. After a few minutes, Sigi Angerer would then say dryly: "That was another stroke of luck." For him, this ritualized dialog was a lengthy speech; he would not normally talk very much. But in fact he was one of the more careful and cautious pilots imaginable. His life's motto as a pilot was: "There are daring pilots—and there are those who survive."

If you give people wings, you encourage them to realize their dreams and ideas, to leave boundaries behind and to surpass themselves. It is only logical that the stories about them should be spread even further. Not just to entertain people, but in order to inspire and infect them with the company's very special DNA. The world of Red Bull is therefore also opened to the world by the Red Bull Media House. In future, magazines like *Red Bulletin* will inform and entertain all those who want to dive deeper into this world. The content produced by Red Bull in the fields of athletics, events and culture is communicated very successfully on external channels as well as the company's own wavelengths. Every year, consumers see billions of Red Bull productions on YouTube, Facebook, and the company's own channels like Servus TV.

The great challenge for the next years will be to cross the interface from Marketing to Media Business. Rather like the introduction of the energy drink, for which Red Bull first had to create a market, the Media House will need to convince with its productions without looking too hard at the quota—in line with Mateschitz's belief that a good product will find its own consumers. That was difficult for the marketing world to understand, and in the media world this task definition has also led to misunderstandings at times. And yet it should all be quite easy: ideas and stories from the world of Red Bull and its protagonists are taken up, placed in a narrative context, produced in exciting form and then broadcast. Preferably on all channels. For some years now, the magazine *Red Bulletin* has been full of surprises with its stories from outside the realms of everyday life about the high-performance achievements of people who go in search of adventure. And with regard to the production of moving pictures, there are already a number of long formats like *The Dawn Wall*, about the extreme climber Tommy Caldwell's conquest of El Capitan, which is not only convincing but which make the viewer hungry for more.

So now, at the end of this first section, let us cast a brief, relatively statistical glance at the success story of Red Bull. Content marketing and the already-described government advertising strengthened each other mutually and over the years gave Red Bull a topicality which drove its revenues figures through the ceiling. The turnover doubled every year between 1987 and 1993. In 1994 it exploded to hit the € 114 million mark; in 2000, it reached the billion-euro level, and rose in 2004 to two billion, to three billion in 2006, four billion in 2010, five billion in 2012, six billion in 2016, seven billion in 2019, and eleven billion in 2022.

Today, Red Bull is one of the largest alcohol-free drinks concerns beside Pepsi and Coca-Cola. In Austria the concern sold more than one *Tray* of Red Bull per head; today every Austrian citizen, whether a newborn baby or an old man, drinks an average of thirty cans of Red Bull per year. With a *Per Capita Consumption (PCC)* of thirty, Red Bull achieves a turnover in Austria of more than € 250 million and shows impressively what is possible in other countries. With revenues of over four billion, the USA is the country with the biggest revenues, but the *PCC* lies only in the medium single-figure range.

Furthermore, the revenues from soft drinks are currently stagnating or declining slightly, while the energy drinks category is demonstrating double-figure growth in most markets. Why, the consumer asks, should I consume so much sugar and so many calories for so little flavor? So he turns instead either to water if thirsty or to Red Bull, in order to improve performance. Both categories demonstrate high growth rates in the relevant Nielsen Charts*, and I am convinced that in the medium term Red Bull will succeed worldwide in achieving something that has already happened in some countries: namely, to replace Coca-Cola as the largest drinks company.

Red Bull gives people and their ideas wings so that they can devote themselves to a project in Viktor Frankl's sense. The increases in revenues and popularity of the Red Bull brand are only the consequence of these efforts, which are being implemented with great passion. Countless numbers of people recognize this and love Red Bull as the expression of a stable value preservation in which product and marketing demonstrate a creative, confident, and unconventional basic attitude.

---

* Nielsen is a market research company which measures what consumers view (*Watch*), for example which advertising or which program, and what they purchase (*Buy*), for example which brands and products.

II

HOW TO GIVE
COMPANIES WINGS

1 VIKTOR FRANKL AS THE PIONEER OF A PRACTICED HUMANISM

// The happiness of those who aspire to be famous depends upon others; the happiness of those who seek pleasure varies with the moods which they cannot control; but the happiness of the wise man grows from what they do of their own free will. //

MARCUS AURELIUS

In the summer of 1944, Viktor Frankl was thirty-nine years old and was interned in Theresienstadt concentration camp. He was about to be transferred to Auschwitz. At this time, his father had already died of starvation and a pulmonary edema in Theresienstadt. Frankl had eased his death "at his own discretion as a doctor" with a vial of morphine which he had smuggled into the camp. Frankl noticed that prisoners had a better chance of surviving if someone or something was waiting for them after their longed-for release from the camp. He imagined that what was waiting for him was his "Life Mountain," the Rax, and the lecturer's desk in a lecture theater at Vienna Adult Education College, where he would report on his experiences:—about what he was currently living through. In his imagination he was giving a lecture with the title *Psychology of the Concentration Camp*, which would explain that even under the most adverse circumstances, people were able to find a purpose in life.

In the summer of 1944, a twenty-one-year-old soldier was serving in the United States army. He had been born in the first generation to a Russian-Jewish immigrant family in New York, and a year later, in April 1945, he would free Frankl from the Türkheim camp. The young soldier's name was Aaron Antonovsky. After the war, he would study sociology at Yale University and—equally influenced by the horrors of war—he would become the father of salutogenesis, a concept that examines the question as to what keeps people healthy.

And finally, in the summer of 1944, a ten-year-old boy was standing on the platform at Budapest station with his mother, two brothers, and about seventy relatives, bidding them farewell before boarding one of the last trains to leave the city for freedom. As the train approached, they could hear the first bombs falling. While the train was steaming towards Venice, where the boy's father, a Hungarian consul in Italy, was waiting for the family in order to travel with them to the United States, shots were fired at the train and the windows shattered. The boy's name was Mihály, and he thought to himself, there must "really be a better way of living than the one here." Mihály Csíkszentmihályi, for that was his full name, would later study psychology at the University of Chicago; during the 1970s he would describe the "Flow Experience," and become one of the founders of the Positive Psychology movement.

So, in that year 1944, Antonovsky was about half as old as Frankl, and Csíkszentmihályi was half as old as Antonovsky, and yet the Second World War had a decisive effect on the work of all three. The war and the concentration camps which cost millions of people their lives, brought Frankl and Antonovsky to consider the same questions: what are the circumstances which allow some people to survive in the face of hunger, cold, torture, the loss of family and friends, and a constant confrontation with the possibility of death? What enables them to "nonetheless say yes to life"? Csíkszentmihályi, too, felt called upon as a result of his experiences to confront the consequences of war with a concept dedicated to the finding of happiness and purpose in life. All three transferred their experiences of the camps and the war to everyday life and examined their theories for their suitability for everyday use.

Without these three pioneers, some of the important developments in modern psychology would have been unthinkable. Frankl, Antonovsky, and Csíkszentmihályi show us ways that not only people, but also organizations and entire societies can be more contented and happier.

Admittedly, Antonovsky did not serve in the precise unit of Texan troops that liberated Frankl from his final camp, Türkheim, on April 27, 1945. However, as a soldier serving in the war on the side of the Allies, he did not remain blind to the horrors of the concentration camp and the war. He had had to interrupt his studies of economics and history at Yale University for military service. After the war he changed, almost by chance, to the subject of medical sociology and completed his studies in 1955 with a doctorate in sociology. After years of teaching and research in New York and Teheran, he emigrated in 1960 to Israel, where he worked in Jerusalem as a medical sociologist at the Institute for Applied Social Research.

While for Frankl his personal experience in and survival of the concentration camp provided the decisive key experience for his further work, for Antonovsky it was an investigation in 1970 into the adaptability of women in the menopause from different ethnic groups who were living in Israel. One group of women in the study had been born in Central Europe between 1914 and 1923, so in 1939 they had been between 16 and 25 years of age. For reasons that Antonovsky "could never quite remember," these women were also asked whether they had been interned in a concentration camp. The fact that 29 percent of the women who had had to suffer through a concentration camp were in good physical and mental shape, led Antonovsky to an "absolute change of direction in his work." It was considerably fewer than in the control group, where 51 percent felt healthy, but for Antonovsky it was a "dramatic experience" to discover that even after the horrors of the camp, the subsequent homelessness, and the experience of three wars in their new homeland Israel, people could feel that they were "in a reasonable state of health."

He decided to devote his research in future to the question as to what enabled people to stay healthy even after the most adverse experiences and events, and to defer the question regarding the causes of illness. Antonovsky thereby took the decisive first step towards a treasure hunt for potentials and away from the pathological search for errors in coping with everyday life. He subsequently developed the salutogenesis model and published his main work *Health, Stress and Coping* in 1979.

Antonovsky states that the critical factor in coping with the demands of life is what he calls the "Sense of Coherence," or *SOC* for short. The stronger this feeling is developed, the greater our resilience towards stress factors will be. He describes the ability of an individual to understand himself and his surroundings, to perceive them as logical and ordered—and not as random, arbitrary and chaotic, as a dimension he calls "comprehensibility." "Manageability" is the willingness to accept challenges and to find an equilibrium between overload and mental underload. People are not reeds in the wind, giving way and resignedly accepting their role as victims, able to be bent at any time. The world is seen not as a burden but as a welcome challenge. It is a feeling that "things will sort themselves out." For Frankl these are the optimistic individuals who are prepared to make choices, to face uncertainty and hazards, who have confidence in themselves and their abilities, and who never simply resign themselves to their fate. They are the opposite of the unlucky devil who doesn't know what is going on, the antonym of the *schlimazel* who gets the soup poured over his best jacket, the sort of person who is always a victim and who quickly blames others for his misfortunes, but never himself.

Antonovsky describes the last and most important component of this sense of coherence as the whole-hearted commitment to something. "Those individuals who according to our classification had a strong *SOC*, always spoke of aspects of life which were important to them, which they cared deeply about, things which in their eyes 'were meaningful'—in the emotional, not only the cognitive meaning of the term ... Shortly after I had written my book, my attention was drawn to Frankl's (1975) work, and there is no doubt that it influenced the choice of term for the description of these components." Referring to Frankl's work, Antonovsky described these components in 1987 in *Unraveling the Mystery of Health: How People Manage Stress and Stay Well* as *Meaningfulness*, and emphasized their central importance. Without commitment and real emotional interest, the other two dimensions are meaningless and become eroded. In other words: without the dedication to "probably ... work and love," failure is pre-programmed, even if we "know the rules of the game ... and believe that we have the resources available to play successfully." On the other hand, people who become involved and committed to or for someone or something, will always find ways to understand their situation and to make means available for the purpose they are pursuing. Without the component of meaning, life will become purposeless and a succession of burdensome and fatiguing episodes, regardless of the surroundings into which we are born or find ourselves.

And so our discussion leads us to Mihály Csíkszentmihályi, and the "Flow Experience" first described by him in 1975. Although at this point he had not yet been influenced by Frankl's works, Csíkszentmihályi chose an empirical approach which was in line with the principles of Frankl, which he had primarily derived from his experience of life, and he also confirmed Frankl's work in his field research. For Frankl, who throughout his life was repeatedly accused of an inadequately scientific attitude, this must have been particularly gratifying. It was also Csíkszentmihályi's aim to make the world a better place, and to contribute to the happiness and well-being of people. He experienced this wish even as a ten-year-old boy in the train that was bombed on the journey to Italy. For him, too, the striving for self-knowledge was the key to a happy life. Without hope and meaning, humankind is left only with its drives; in other words, like animals, all efforts would be focused on the search for food, safety, and procreation, and they would lack the specifically human, the will for meaning. In order to overcome the hunt for happiness and to surpass oneself, individuals must give themselves an "evocative pattern," develop their potential, make full use of their talents, and embark on a "trajectory of personal development and increasingly emotional, cognitive and social complexity." In Csíkszentmihályi's work this lasting vision draws its strength from the soul: "From the energy which an individual or organization focuses on goals which point beyond themselves." Here we also find in Csíkszentmihályi's work the "self transcendency" of Frankl, which is so aptly described with the verbal image of the eye whose ability to perceive paradoxically depends on the fact that it cannot see itself. For Csíkszentmihályi, this "Transcending [becomes] possible through the *Flow Experience* [and] consequently offers us the rare chance to actively engage with something that is bigger than ourselves, without having to dispense with the potential that is present in the area of the intellect, the body, and our own will." At this point, Csíkszentmihályi also refers to Frankl: "Half a century ago, the Austrian psychiatrist Viktor Frankl wrote 'that we cannot achieve happiness by wishing to be happy—happiness must occur as the non-intentional consequence of working towards a goal that is greater than the individual himself.' Our own findings show clearly how true this observation is."

Csíkszentmihályi carried out thousands of interviews and questioned people from all professions and walks of life regarding the circumstances in which they would experience complete immersion and a total absorption in a specific task. We are most likely to experience this feeling when we are challenged neither too much nor too little, in other words when we are subjected to the right level of stress. The task will not make us fail, but neither is it too monotonous.

The "Flow Experience" has very little to do with comfort and luxury. Rather, "Flow" describes great effort and performance on our part, often under austere conditions. Fun and consumption are on the whole detrimental to this feeling. Hedonistic materialism is accordingly not a good breeding ground for "Flow" and it will not come as a surprise that an excessive interest in money and pleasure tend to be detrimental to happiness and well-being. As a consequence, therefore, we should distinguish between the pleasure which we experience in the striving for long-term perfection of our own abilities and skills, and the short-term pleasures that our consumer society offers. Adverse circumstances, on the other hand, can even foster a "Flow Experience."

The protagonist in Stefan Zweig's *The Royal Game: A Chess Story* finds himself in such a situation, for example. He is put into solitary confinement by the Gestapo and is completely cut off from the outside world in a hotel room of the Metropol on Morzinplatz in Vienna, which at the same time is the headquarters of the Gestapo in Vienna. After a vacuum lasting for weeks, a "constructed, complete nothingness," he is able to purloin a book and take it to his room. At first he is greatly disappointed to discover that it is a chess review. But before long the book provides nourishment for his starved intellect. He plays the games it describes move by move, his absolute concentration focused on the next move or next sequence of moves. (Only later in the tale do we learn that it is not possible to want to win against yourself when playing chess without becoming schizophrenic.) In the "Flow" experience, the way is the goal. We are calmly occupied by something, at complete ease, but totally alert; this is not a time of focused attention, but of absorption in the activity. The *Feedback* follows immediately; during the course of his efforts to understand the games, the first-person narrator becomes an expert and can re-enact them "with his eyes closed."

The tale is a perfect example of the "dynamic nature" of the "Flow." Demands and abilities are adapted to each other step by step and raised until the narrator reaches a degree of perfection which—as we learn towards the end of the story—is world-class in the game against Mirko Czentovic, the world chess champion of the time. The "creative passion" (Kurt Hahn) and the focusing on the game make the narrator forget everything else around him. He loses himself, as it were, in his actions; he distances himself from himself and thus from his own fears and compulsions. This, more or less, is how it feels when something outstanding is created, when talent encounters enthusiasm and diligence, whether in sport, at work, or in art.

The "archetype of the individual in flow" is a child playing. The reward lies in the game itself; it requires no particular external motivation such as praise or admiration. No one forces the child to play; it will play of its own accord. The child will decide autonomously what it will play, and with whom. In playing, and in the choice of game and the question as to whether to play alone or with friends, the child intuitively follows its inclinations and potential. Here, we find valuable hints of talents which can later be developed into strengths and mastery. The child will generally choose tasks that it can comfortably master, tasks that neither bore it nor overwhelm it. No one has to tell the child that the tower is standing or the sandcastle has collapsed. The information regarding success or failure comes from the game itself, and is thus "a direct consequence." The child concentrates entirely on the moment, progresses one step at a time and forgets in its total commitment to the task, not only itself but also the time, so that it may not hear its parent calling that supper is ready. The child is utterly convinced that what it is doing is important. A "Flow Experience" of this kind contributes to making sure that the strokes of fate which life has in store for us may "injure us, but will not conquer us."

Frankl, Antonovsky, and Csíkszentmihályi form a philosophical triumvirate whose foundation lies in the individual's search for meaning. The precondition for a successful, happy life is a life full of meaning, in which we decide freely and autonomously on a goal and choose our tasks. We shape our surroundings, give of our best, and if the situation cannot be changed, we still have the option of changing our attitude. What brings us closer to meaningfulness is good, and what distracts us from it is bad. Our conscience will serve here as compass.

Individuals bear within themselves the means to achieve this goal. These are our talents, which must be recognized and developed. Trusting in the potential that is dormant in each and every one of us, we are called upon to appreciate our talents through diligence and practice and to develop our strengths. The better we succeed in this, the more we defy the adverse circumstances which life has in store for all of us, the greater will be our achievements.

The consequence is the fulfillment of tasks while oblivious to all around us. It is the dedication to something that is greater than ourselves; it enables us not to regard ourselves as so important and to free ourselves from fears and constraints. The fulfillment of tasks by which we forget ourselves therefore means self-transcendency and distancing ourselves from ourselves at the same time. We recognize this state in that when we are intently concentrating on a task, the world will seem to us to be both comprehensible and shapeable.

In this respect we could also say that Frankl's "Will to Meaning," Antonovsky's "Salutogenesis," and Csíkszentmihályi's "Flow" form the framework of a not necessarily utopian working world, in which workers are called upon to live autonomously, to make full use of their potential, to turn their talents into strengths, to experience "Flow" as often as possible, and to be prepared to forget themselves in committing themselves to a specific, meaningful task: to put it simply, to give of "their best." It is evident that work can be meaningful. The contribution the worker may make in such an environment is his greatest reward.

From talent to strength to purpose — a personal treasure hunt

> *"* There is one thing, and only one, in the whole universe which we know more about than we could learn from external observation. That one thing is Man. We do not merely observe men, we are men. In this case we have, so to speak, inside information; we are in the know. *"*
>
> C. S. LEWIS

Some time ago Stefan Salzer, our Global Head of Human Resources, and I conducted a job interview with the son of an employee who had worked for Red Bull for many years. The applicant was born in 1992, the same year as my daughter. The Red Bull Wingfinder Test (which we shall describe in greater detail in due course) revealed that his strengths included being "open to new ideas, innovative, analytical, and gregarious." The elegant young man sitting facing us in a smart suit felt that these qualities characterized him well: his interests focused on the one hand on art and fashion, indicating a pronounced sense of aesthetics, and on the other on data analysis, which he found easy thanks to his ability to think rapidly and precisely. He had graduated as a Bachelor and Master of Science at the EBS University in Germany; in his Bachelor's and Master's dissertations he had analyzed the art market for investments and cryptocurrencies and had also completed internships at Hugo Boss and UBS.

The young man looked as if he would have a promising future ahead of him. All the same, there was still one thing that was tormenting him. He could not make up his mind in favor of one single talent: data analysis, or would he perhaps prefer aesthetics after all? After a few weeks he had felt under-stretched at both Hugo Boss and UBS, which had continued to unsettle him. During his conversation with us he made the impression of being almost in despair because he was not sure which direction to choose. The fashion sector or investment banking, or possibly an academic career instead, an option which a famous university in Italy had offered him? Gazing frequently at the ground and in a state of permanent self-reflection, he told us of his considerations, inclinations, and doubts. Eventually I had had enough and told him that his education and practical experience meant that he was ideally qualified, that his talents would open up a wide range of opportunities in life as a knowledge worker, and that all he had to do was to decide on which field. If I were his father, I would forbid him to continue to brood any longer over himself, his career, and his salary opportunities.

Many young people are like this applicant. They ask themselves: What shall I study? Which career shall I choose? In which company? Which jobs shall I apply for? What will my duties there be, and what is my goal? And ultimately all these questions lead to one decisive point: In which context will I have the opportunity to develop and use my talents as fully as possible?

Before we turn to the connection between the finding of talent, choice of career, and strength-oriented management, I should like to go in search of clues. What is a talent? Is it something we are born with, that we inherit from our ancestors? Does it crystallize during the early years of our life? How can the talent be developed into a strength with which we can produce outstanding performances? And how can this become meaningful, not only in theoretical-philosophical terms, but in a business environment?

For each of these questions I shall turn to advisors, three people whose actions will put us on the right track and who will bring us a step further in the individual stages in the development of talent on the path towards meaning.

Let us begin with the question regarding the genetic requirements. Dr. Eckart von Hirschhausen gained his doctorate *summa cum laude* and comes from an old family of academics from the German Baltic region. He initially studied medicine and worked as a doctor in pediatric neurology at the Freie Universität Berlin. However, he was obviously not in the right place to develop his talents; today he is a successful presenter and cabaret artist. When asked why he exchanged the hospital for the stage, he says: "Creativity is my strength and my great flaw. That means not doing everything according to plan, improvising, bringing things together again and again in unexpected ways. That is not a good idea in a hospital. And I love to express myself freely, to make things up, to play with language. That is not a good idea in doctor's letters or prescriptions either. On stage I can use much more of what I am, what I know, what I can do, and what I can give. I have more fun, and others have more fun with me. I am in my element, in the flow, in a live situation!"

We are born with special gifts, be they cognitive, artistic, or physical. Some are obvious. In his "Medizinisches Kabarett"* (Medical Cabaret), Hirschhausen points out that penguins look clumsy on land, but that they seem to glide effortlessly through the water. With wings that have evolved into flippers, breastbone shaped like the keel of a boat, upper and lower armbones that are firmly fused together, and webbing, the penguin is perfectly adapted to life in the water. It spends longer periods on land only for reproductive purposes and to care for its young. There it can only waddle because of its stiff knee joints and its legs that are attached at the back. In any case, Hirschhausen felt sorry for the penguin that he saw in a zoo in Norway:

> "I felt sorry for it: Do you have to wear that tuxedo? Where's your waist, then? And above all: Did God forget your knees? I had already reached my verdict: Faulty design. And then I took another look through the glass panel into the penguins' swimming pool. Suddenly 'my' penguin leapt into the water and swam right up to my face. Anyone who has ever seen penguins under water is simply speechless. It was in its element! A penguin is ten times more streamlined than a Porsche! With a liter

---

* See *hirschhausen.com/glueck*.

of gas it would be able to travel the equivalent of over 2,500 kilometers! They are excellent swimmers and hunters, and they can dance in the water! And I thought: 'Faulty design!' ... We all have our strengths and our weaknesses. Many people try for ages to eliminate their weak points. If you improve your weaknesses you will be at best mediocre. But if you strengthen your strengths you will be unique. And those who are not like the others can take comfort: There are plenty of others! ... People only rarely succeed in changing themselves completely and fundamentally. If you were born a penguin, even seven years of psychotherapy will not turn you into a giraffe. So don't waste your time refusing to accept your fate: If you are a penguin, don't stay in the steppe. Take one small step at a time and find your water. And then: Jump in! And swim! And you will know what it means to be in your element."

Hirschhausen presents the example of the penguin in a bold and entertaining manner, and yet here he is only describing the obvious genetic preconditions of body structure, which anyone can understand. Nobody would even dream of ignoring the question of height for a basketball player. Science is already much further than that. The basic requirement for top performance, for example, in sports calling for strength and the ability to sprint is that the skeletal muscles can produce strength rapidly. And that, in turn, is genetically pre-programmed. Several genetic variants have been identified which are responsible for exceptional strength and sprinting ability. In Australia, only those athletes are accepted into the training squad who have the correct genetic requirements. Genetics also play a role in cognitive and artistic talents. In music, perfect pitch—the ability to determine precisely the pitch of what has been heard—is determined genetically. Those who have talent for something, for a task or with a specific material, will be responsive in that field from an early age.

Now we must ask the question as to how these talents become evident. And that leads us directly to Wolfgang Amadeus Mozart. The composer's creative work and activities are perhaps the best embodiment of talent development. On the one hand, Mozart had outstanding musical talent. Joseph Haydn assured Leopold Mozart in 1785, after he had heard the string quartet dedicated to him: "I say to you before God, as an honest man, your son is the greatest composer I have ever met or whose name I know: He has taste and great knowledge of composition."

Salzburg's genius had perfect pitch, so that he became familiar with music from an early age. And he was born into a musical family. His father Leopold was the court composer at the court of the Archbishop of Salzburg. His son absorbed and wrote down all the music he encountered. He had no difficulty imitating various styles of composition. In contrast to his great rival Salieri, however, he did not only imitate others. Taking familiar works as a starting point, Mozart developed his own sophisticated style. Amongst other features, the length and complexity of his works increased; wind instruments acquired an independent character that had hitherto been unknown, and in his operas he created convincing psychological-dramaturgical character portraits. In his music Mozart succeeded in "combining the apparently light and catchy with the musically difficult and demanding."* Mozart

---

* See wolfgang-amadeus.at.

composed, as it says in a letter dated December 16, 1780, "Music for people of all kinds ... but not for those with long ears."

This irrepressible interest in music was evident from his earliest years. "Wolferl," as he was known, traveled as a wunderkind with his sister Maria Anna—"Nannerl"—from court to court throughout Europe and enchanted the noblemen with the sonatas he had composed for piano and violin. Mozart wrote his first symphony before he was ten years old. He dedicated his entire brief life to music and his compositions. His operas with the libretti by Lorenzo da Ponte are immortal. Composed with pleasure-oriented lightness, they are perhaps the very epitome of how close a man can come to the divine. And anyone who has heard the *Great Mass in C minor*, which is played every year in St. Peter's monastery church within the framework of the Salzburg Festival, where it was performed for the first time in 1782 with Mozart's sister Nannerl at the piano, will understand the timelessness and uniqueness of Mozart's compositions.

Mozart died shortly before his thirty-sixth birthday in Vienna of a "severe miliary fever." His partly unfinished *Requiem* is musical testimony to his self-sacrifice to his music. Mozart's talent thrust itself upon him and took possession, as it were, of his person. Born into a musical family and equipped with perfect pitch, Mozart gave his genius free rein and created in an Orphic frenzy the works which eternally delight and move not only us but also the generations to come.

Christoph Willibald Gluck, a friend of Mozart's and his predecessor as "Imperial Chamber Composer" at the Viennese Court, was one of the most important German composers of operas during the eighteenth century. For Gluck, too, it was clear from childhood onwards which direction his talent would take him in. But unlike Mozart, Gluck's ancestors on his father's side were all foresters. His father wanted him to take up this profession and had determined from an early age that he should become his successor. In his memoirs of his youth, Gluck describes his drive to make music: "My entire thoughts and aspirations were focused entirely on music, and forestry was pushed to the side. Since this did not correspond with my father's wishes, he supervised my work with great strictness and doubled the amount in order to keep me from a trade which, as he said, would never be able to feed me. So I practiced at night; but that disturbed the quiet in the house and my father's rest, and he locked my instruments away. Such was my enthusiasm for music that I took up the noisy Jew's harp, which I played with great skill within a short space of time; but I was happiest on Sundays in the church choir." With courage and against all conventions and the opposition of his family, Gluck defied his apparently sealed fate of becoming a forester.

The unique talent of Franz Kafka, a writer who has left us some of the greatest works of world literature, was totally wasted in the profession in which he earned a living. He experienced his work as a lawyer and insurance assessor as pure boredom, and he described it in a letter to his friend Milena Jesenská as "ludicrous and easy … I don't know why they pay me." The hours spent in the office were torture and the last minute of work a "springboard into amusement." Writing was his passion. If Kafka were alive today, we could wish him the Nobel Prize for Literature, and that he would be able to live from his books.

All three followed their talent, but what a difference in the quality of their decision regarding their chosen career! Mozart's path was predestined from the beginning, Gluck resisted the expectations of his family, and Kafka surrendered to his fate, at least with regard to earning a living, and pursued his passion, writing, only in his leisure time. And yet all three remain immortal in their works: the world would not be the same without *Queen of the Night, Dance of the Furies,* and *Metamorphosis.*

So now we come to the question as to how to develop talents and strengths. In the mid-1990s I traveled to Vienna on numerous occasions with my friend Martin Hengstschläger to attend further education events for lawyers. Since the events ran over two days, we spent the night at the flat of his younger brother Markus. Markus Hengstschläger had studied genetics at the University of Vienna and had carried out research at Yale University in the United States. He was the youngest university professor at the medical school in Vienna, where he is the head of the Institute for Medical Genetics today. He is a scientist who has won numerous awards and who has an international reputation. He teaches students and works in the fields of genetic diagnostics, foundational research, and innovation consultancy. Hengstschläger is also the author of three best-sellers that reached the top of the charts (*Die Macht der Gene, Endlich unendlich,* and *Die Durchschnittsfalle*). Above all, however, he is a gifted speaker who gives lectures and interviews in which he entertains and fascinates his audience with insight into genetics and the search for talent.

He likes to use the following story as the starting point for his remarks. Imagine that your child comes home from school with a report listing top marks in German and a mark in math that is only adequate. You will probably ask first of all how many other children had the same mark—or even a worse one—in math. If many of them had the same mark or worse, you will probably relax to a certain degree. But woe betide if hardly any had such poor marks. In this case the holidays will probably be spent with a surge in extra lessons in math. You will ignore the German mark, because the child clearly has no difficulties there. There is a danger that the extra work will be devoted to the weak points, and the child's strengths will be neglected.

School is a place where unfortunately all too often the emphasis lies on the search for mistakes and where negative feedback can lead to resignation. Schools have the task of teaching children the basic skills of reading, writing, and arithmetic, which are regarded as the basic requirements for a knowledge worker in our service society. For this reason, children simply have to put in a certain amount of effort, and sometimes that also means having to work at their own weaknesses. A good teacher will try to minimize the weaknesses and at the same time to encourage talent, in order not to discourage the child. Like my math and sports teacher, whom I still meet with every year to play cards. When my mother drove 200 kilometers from Linz to the boarding school in Saalfelden to attend the parents' day and arrived feeling sick because her brand-new VW Beetle had a leaking tank and smelled of gas, Professor Heribert Tollich suggested that she should rest for a while on his couch. And what about my son, asked my indisposed mother. "Don't worry. He's no genius in math, but he'll pass." My mother rested for an hour and then drove back home again, reassured. My teacher was right: Math was never my strong point, but I preferred to focus on German, Sport, History, and Geography.

There are no sportspeople, artists, or even "only" knowledge workers who achieve top performances and who have not also worked hard to overcome their weaknesses. Who have not failed dozens—or even hundreds—of times at the same place and who then got up again, carried on, and continued to try and try again, until they succeeded at last. That does not mean that we should set out to search for the errors. We basically work on something we are good at, but we perfect it. That is not always a piece of cake, but the result of these efforts will bring us, more than anything else in the world, satisfaction, fulfillment, and a sense of purpose.

The most efficient form of learning takes place through positive and negative feedback, whereby the former should outweigh the latter. The positive feedback will motivate us and fill us with new energy, while we remember the negative feedback better and it is this which will help us to grow. Good trainers make sure a training unit always ends with the experience of success or positive feedback. Marcial Losada, the former Director of the Center for Advanced Research (CFAR) in Ann Arbor, Michigan, carried out numerous studies on the dynamics of interaction and the productivity of business teams. He investigated the relationship between positive and negative feedback and the effectiveness of team work by means of critical performance indicators such as productivity and customer satisfaction. Although there was criticism of his concept of the ratio of critical positivity (¾ positive and ¼ negative, also known as the Losada line), it can nonetheless be regarded as certain that the most successful teams received both positive and negative feedback. To receive only positive or only negative feedback is detrimental to performance.

And yet, we basically work too frequently in error mode. To concentrate on error in our work is the opposite of empowerment and lays the foundations for a collective victimology, in which we see ourselves as "nothing but victims." Searching for errors makes us operate in sickness mode. We avoid effort and take refuge from our miserable everyday lives. Our self-esteem is at an all-time low. Countless working and life relationships are destroyed by self-pity, accusations of blame, frustration, and annoyance. Then all that we hope for in our lives is that we will not plummet down to rock bottom and that we can at least remain average. The ideal we strive to achieve is relaxation and passivity. And indeed: in the short term, consumption and entertainment will distract us and camouflage our feeling of emptiness. In the long term, however, the result will be anger, fear, neuroses, and depression. Mental illness has reached epidemic proportions. Nowadays, depression occurs ten times more frequently than it did fifty years ago, and the prevalence of this illness during a person's life (the average point at which it occurs) has halved and now lies at approximately fifteen years. This leads to the waste of considerable social resources.*

To conclude this first section, let us summarize the whole in an image once more: Talents are like highways in the brain. On the highways of our gifts we will find our specific tasks faster and more easily than away from the road in the

---

* The general psychology sector follows this trend. Science continues to focus predominantly on people's negative sides and shows their inadequacies in a variety of ways. Even though Positive Psychology tries hard to provide help, today only few contributions are devoted to possibilities and the search for potential. The evaluation of thirty years of publications on psychology results in some 6,000 articles on anger, 42,000 articles on fear, and 54,000 articles on depression. On the other side, 415 articles were written on the subject of joy, 1,700 articles on happiness, and 2,500 articles on satisfaction. In the words of Abraham Maslow, it is as if psychology voluntarily restricts itself to just one half of its tasks, namely the dark side.

thicket and quagmire of our weaknesses. As is generally known, these will lead at best to mediocrity or to what Hengstschläger calls the "trap of the average." Each individual has his or her own gifts, and it is their responsibility to find these talents, to cultivate them, and to transform them into strengths. Society, family, school, and the world of work are under the obligation to provide support in the unearthing of this treasure.

If we now pursue the path from the talents which have been revealed and developed into strengths as far as the work context, to our choice of career, then at the beginning of every choice lies the will to take our fate into our own hands. But does it really exist, this often-evoked and yet controversial free will? "The whole work of man seems to consist in nothing but proving to himself every minute that he is a man and not a piano key," writes Dostoevsky in *Notes from Underground*. In order not to be a 'piano key,' it takes two types of freedom: social freedom and individual freedom. Socially we expend our energy in supporting equal opportunities for as many people as possible. Even if we only succeed to a certain extent, compared with the past we live today—at least in Western democracies—in greater freedom than ever before.

We should see—in a historical and social context—the observation from Viktor Frankl that "human behavior is not dictated by conditions which people encounter, but by decisions which they take themselves". Because it is not a matter of course that we can choose freely our career, our partner, or even where we live. Throughout the Middle Ages and until the early modern period, people were not free, and their choices were very limited. Not for months or years, but throughout their lives and across the generations. In Salzburg, the Archbishop was the local ruler, and until well into the eighteenth century he had to give his permission for someone to move somewhere else, to another town and hence into the jurisdiction of another ruler. Citizens were required to pay taxes to the local ruler, and if they moved he would lose income from their taxes. Occupations were determined by birth. Unmarried children had no civic rights and hence no access to the occupations governed by the guilds or even to a position a court. They were limited to occupations as servants and lower-paid wage laborers. The choice of a partner took place exclusively within one's own social class and was arranged by one's parents.

Perhaps that is why, for Martin Luther, man was still entirely the instrument of God. The unruly "peasant spirit" was convinced that man's fate lay entirely in the hand of God and that his "enslaved will" was only free when he was doing wrong. Erasmus von Rotterdam contradicted him. He welcomed the 95 Theses and agreed with Luther on the subject of the sale of indulgences, but he wanted to see Christendom united and not split. The humanist strove for unity and peace, not for discord and hatred, which was why he was strongly opposed to the intransigent attitude of Luther, which he supported with his theses and for which he was prepared to risk war. In the end he felt compelled to take up a position against Luther. In 1524, Erasmus chose his subject carefully: *De libero arbitrio*, his work on free will. Erasmus shared the opinion of Socrates, who is said to have stated before drinking the hemlock: "I do not know whether God will approve our deeds. But we have certainly tried to please him."

When we read a statement like this, we can only say: "Holy Socrates, intercede for us!" The idea of an individual who endeavors to give of his best and who voluntarily does good seems to Luther to commit blasphemy and is repulsive: "I cannot describe the repulsion I felt upon reading this little book on free will." Erasmus would be proved right; the schism in the Church was sealed at the Diet of Augsburg in 1530, and one hundred years later, half Germany was razed to the ground for thirty years. And yet, Erasmus was the prince of science and the supreme humanist who, as forerunner of the Enlightenment, helped to steer Europe towards Liberty, Equality, and Fraternity.

The construct of individual free will remains controversial even in the twenty-first century. Jürgen Sandkühler, the head of the Brain Research Center in Vienna, is convinced that humans have no free will, and finds that this concept is "almost insignificant." For the individual, it makes no difference whether he is really free or succumbs to the illusion of freedom. Because a decision made of one's own free will can be neither proven nor refuted, free will remains "the wondrous creature," which at present in any case has not been proven scientifically. For Sandkühler, decisions are a consequence of constrained biological, physical, and chemical processes in the brain; for him, a free will which does not follow these physical laws cannot be proven. And ultimately even the complex biochemical and neuronal processes remain unpredictable and scientifically contentious.

"If we are no longer in a position to change a situation, we are [still] called upon to change ourselves," wrote Viktor Frankl. The determinism supported by Sandkühler is a minority opinion. The majority of philosophers today share Frankl's view that the individual is free to make decisions in harmony with his or her values and convictions, even if biology, hereditary disposition, and environmental influences influence these decisions. The individual, equipped with the intellectual power to disagree, remains unpredictable and *agens,* and consequently more than "nothing but *reagens.*"

Markus Hengstschläger sees things similarly. He is convinced that humans cannot be reduced to their genes. Their genes are "only pencil and paper; each of us writes our history ourselves." How the cards have been distributed; what can be ascribed to genes and what to free will and the environment, remains a movable system and is not the same for any two people. "How much talent is inherited and what influence our surroundings have, is probably the question which is most actively discussed. I say: People cannot under any circumstances be reduced to their genes as regards their talents. Without practice, nothing is possible. But practice will not have the same result for each of us—because each of is us genetically unique."

Each human being is different and this individuality is, as we have learned, a good thing. At this point, Hengstschläger tells another story: There are many individuals swimming in a pond. Environmental conditions then make the water temperature in the pond rise a little. If all the inhabitants of the pond were absolutely identical and not equipped to cope with the new environmental conditions, they would all die. But if the pond-dwellers are all different individuals, a selection process would take place and very probably some of them would survive. And that is precisely what happened in the history of evolution. The dinosaurs became extinct but the mammals survived. Humans are the summit of this development; they not only adapt genetically, but they also built caves, houses, and by now inter-galactic spaceships, in order to be able to defy changes in environmental conditions. Admittedly, humans today also produce 300 million tonnes of plastic annually, have already processed half a billion cubic meters of concrete, and ignited more than 500 nuclear explosive devices. Let us hope that we survive the Anthropocene, in which Man as a force of nature has already moved more of the Earth's crust than all the winds and rivers combined. In a so-called world that is complex, unsafe, and constantly on the move—the experts use the term VUCA world to describe it (for *volatility, uncertainty, complexity,* and *ambiguity)*, individuality and difference form in any case our best reinsurance. And so it is essential to encourage diversity and not to prevent it.

A doctrinaire determinist may insist that free will is an illusion but, ultimately, this is neither provable nor disprovable. Maybe this is similar to quantum theory, where observation influences reality. For others of us—and this includes Viktor Frankl and Dietrich Mateschitz—we do not experience ourselves as being simply the effects of causes; we experience ourselves as free agents, choosing to paint the canvasses of our lives with whatever materials we can find or make.

Once we are convinced that free choice is real and not an illusion, and that our uniqueness is our greatest strength, then continued self-knowledge is the most important precondition for a good decision. Self-knowledge means becoming aware of our development opportunities and recognizing our natural limitations. Opportunities and limitations are related to each other like Yin and Yang; they are antagonists and yet they are mutually conditional. In striving to take advantage of our opportunities, we reach for the stars, but we must also overcome difficulties and confront our fears and compulsions. To put it another way: Strengths must be encouraged and weaknesses marginalized. Those who do not know their strengths and weaknesses cannot work on them. The better we understand our own strengths and limitations, the better will be our decisions when choosing an occupation and making career decisions. And the more consciously we make these decisions, the more likely we are to love our work and its fruits. So when considering self-awareness, it is a question of nothing less than looking into the mirror and correctly assessing oneself as an individual—of examining things in depth and understanding the history our lives represent and which we write day by day.

If self-knowledge is not to stop at reflection but to lead to a decision, the decisive characteristics will be composure and watchfulness. Serene composure, also known as the Socratic virtue *sophrosyne*, can be described as "maintaining mental equanimity." People who are composed are relaxed, calm, and collected, and are generally healthier and happier as they go through life.* Only someone who is composed and not self-centered, who has achieved maturity through their tasks in life, will be able to achieve true self-knowledge. Composure allows us to confess to fears and mistakes and to admit that there are still things that we need to learn. People who are calm do not insist on being right at any price, but remain open to what is new and see the world as full of possibilities which they can shape. So Frankl's

---

* Anton Pelinka noted in *Radiokolleg* on February 6, 2020, that we also find calm people, regardless of their attitude, more likeable; whether they lean to the left or the right, are conservative or progressive, we welcome people who are composed and, to adapt freely Julius Caesar's observation, we can state: let me be surrounded with calm people!

optimistic individual is therefore always a calm individual. The calm individual affirms life, assumes responsibility, and stands by decisions. Calm individuals make a contribution; for them, life has meaning. It is not other people who are guilty, but they are guilty themselves, and they see strokes of fate as part of life. It is only this stoicism which permits us to accept ourselves in our imperfection, and yet to have a positive worldview of ourselves and our surroundings. Thus, calmness is a valid model against narcissism, alarmism, and the notorious agitation of our time.

The second characteristic that is essential for self-knowledge is watchfulness—watchfulness in order to distinguish between talent and distraction. Let us assume I like reading and playing chess. The mere fact that I enjoy doing something does not necessarily mean that I possess talent in this direction. The fact that I am a passionate reader does not necessarily make me a good author, speaker, or even just a literary critic. Fredmund Malik points out that what we like doing is not necessarily the decisive factor. There is no causal connection between the things that we like doing and those in which we are able to achieve an outstanding performance.

And let us further assume that I not only *enjoy* playing chess, but that I also find it *easy* to think through the possible course of various games, to develop strategies, and to implement them tactically in such a way that I am often better than many of my opponents in the chess club. This would seem to indicate that I possibly possess a talent in the field of logical-analytical thinking, and that, if I continue to play chess seriously, play frequently, study openings and moves, there is a distinct possibility that I could become an excellent player.

To take up the image of the highway again: on the talent highway, our commitment is increased. We experience a desire to focus on a task, to follow an inclination, and to concentrate on a specific material. We have no difficulty focusing on the subject because we find it easy and because we have no difficulty with it. And so we enjoy it and pursue it frequently. Then we must ask ourselves what we do quite naturally, perhaps almost en passant, where we enjoy our greatest successes, and what we were doing when we look back at the best day in recent months. What do others praise us for (or even envy us)? After which activities do we feel fulfilled and on top of the world?

If we find something easy, there is a risk that we will disregard it and pay too little attention to our potential. School, parents, and later we ourselves should therefore pay particular attention to special gifts and encourage and develop them. Because precisely here, on the border between "enjoying something" and "finding it easy," lies the boundary between leisure pursuit and work. Everywhere we are more consumer than producer, we will not exert ourselves, will not cross boundaries, will not even focus on performance. It is the provoking situation in an encroaching world that enables us to grow, step by step. It doesn't happen when we seek distraction, but only when we devote ourselves seriously to a task.

So in the following it is a matter of allowing our talents which have been developed into strengths to blossom in a task, to surpass ourselves and in this way to discover a sense of purpose. The allegory of the three stonemasons and their construction of a cathedral illustrates this point and has taken its place in management training programs.

The story is attributed to Michelangelo: A man arrives on a building site on which three stonemasons are working. It is not possible to distinguish between them as regards appearance. He goes up to the first one and asks: "What are you doing there?" The stonemason looks at him in a puzzled manner and says: "I'm earning my living. I have a wife and six children to support." So the man goes on and comes to the second stonemason. He asks him the same question. The stonemason looks at him proudly and says: "I am the best stonemason in the country." Then the man reaches the last stonemason. He considers the question for a moment and then answers: "I am helping to build a cathedral."

For the third stonemason, his work has a significance and a purpose. He has a "What for" in his work, not just a "Why" like the other two. The third stonemason experiences meaning in his work, and he modestly sees his work as subordinate to the higher goal. The other two were working for a purpose, for money or fame. Peter Drucker finds that only he is the true manager, and he warns us of the second, the "blinkered specialist," who might easily miss the overarching goal. Only those who not only build a cathedral but also forget themselves in their dedication to the task, will experience fulfillment and mastery, the so-called successful life that will leave its mark not only on their surroundings but perhaps even on posterity. That is the only way to become immune to existential crises and burn-out, because the purpose is stronger than any goal, and talent, strengths, and flow are promising ingredients for masterpieces of every kind.

Even as a student, I noticed that those students who had a goal to aim for, found it easier to complete their course of study. This goal made it easier for them to successfully overcome the long haul which every course of study contains—

be it one or more failed exams, or a difficult or uninteresting subject. Their sights were set on something after the completion of their studies: either a powerful career wish or the idea of a particular task. Thus I had always wanted to be a lawyer and to use the knowledge I had acquired to help people. By contrast, the students who were studying simply because of a certain inclination for or general interest in a subject found it much harder to stay the course, so that even minor setbacks or disappointments might lead them to abandon their studies or change to a different subject.

I realize that this observation is purely anecdotal, but it directs our attention toward the aspects which are often ignored in the development from talent to strength. Talents must be used in the service of goals and tasks, and working on our talent requires effort, sacrifice, and the overcoming of our weaker selves. That also applies in our work. According to Don Clifton (whom we shall meet in detail in the next chapter), talents are "naturally occurring patterns of thoughts, feelings, and behavior," in which we must invest. The investment consists of practicing untiringly and adding skills and knowledge to the talent, so that the talent can become a strength. Otherwise, at some stage, diligence will beat talent, as Markus Hengstschläger succinctly pointed out.

Those who have a goal and a task, are more resilient than those who are only interested in money and status. Even though talent is the precondition for outstanding achievements, without a goal to aim for, for which it is worth getting up every day and overcoming obstacles, we shall fail to do justice to our possibilities, let alone achieve outstanding performances and perfection. In addition to what we can hope will be many flow experiences, we shall also always have to pass through the vale of tears, to overcome our fears and defy our despair. Those who are not prepared to accept that will fail to pass muster: they will be weighed and found wanting. Whenever there is talk of building up strengths, this always means in the first instance, to strive through our concentrated efforts and practice for something that is bigger than ourselves: either a task or a goal. In real life, fulfilling tasks is not monocausal and simple, but highly complex and dynamic, which is why we must grow constantly and adapt, reinvent ourselves if necessary, and surpass ourselves. Only in the context of the task does the treasure hunt for talent have meaning.

To take up the pictorial allegory of the cathedral again, we can also say: when faith in the meaningful nature of the task forms the foundation, then talent and strengths are the structure that is erected on that foundation. The better we succeed in applying our strengths, the more beautiful, powerful, and higher the structure will be, that is dedicated not to ourselves, but to something higher. It is not a matter of being the world's best in a discipline in order to experience *flow* and to give a task meaning. Our own strengths are simply waiting to be applied productively. While only we can discover the purpose, the questions concerning talent and strengths are easy, albeit far from trivial. It is a question of a skill which can easily be learned with the right tools.

In their capacity as tools, talent, strength, and flow are basically neutral as regards values. In fact, even the search for meaning is neutral too; only our actions are not neutral. Where we find a purpose, and what we apply our talents to, remains our volition and is hence a question of conscience.

What we dedicate ourselves to is what matters. Each socialization, whether conservative or liberal, every religious creed, be it Christian or Islamic, every milieu, be it humanistic or criminal—indeed, every situation, from gulag to jungle camp, permits the individual to decide. To the best of their knowledge and belief, decent or not. Whatever the decision we are called upon to make may look like, we must take sides—with our "sense organ," our conscience.

2 MARTIN SELIGMAN, DON CLIFTON, AND THE INVENTION OF THE STRENGTH TEST

// Even today, remarkably few Americans are prepared to select jobs for themselves. When you ask, 'Do you know what you are good at? Do you know your strengths?,' most people look at you with a blank stare. Or they often respond in terms of subject knowledge, which is fundamentally the wrong answer. When they prepare their C.V., they still try to list positions like rungs on a ladder. It is time to stop thinking about jobs and career paths, and to accept tasks one after the other. //

PETER DRUCKER

In the United States, happiness research is inextricably linked with the names of Martin Seligman and Gallup (to which we will come later). Martin Seligman researches and teaches at the University of Pennsylvania, where he leads the Positive Psychology Center. He has written fifteen books and hundreds of specialist publications about motivation and personality. In 2011, he was even nominated for the Nobel Peace Prize. Seligman describes himself as a clinical psychologist and is a representative of American Behaviorism.

Until the mid-1990s, the focus of American psychology lay almost exclusively on the prevention and healing of illnesses. Seligman, too, worked initially in the field of prevention, supported by the National Institute for Mental Health, which, contrary to its name, makes funds available almost exclusively for the research into illness. By his own admission, Seligman spent the first thirty years of his career researching misery.

In 1996, he was elected President of the American Psychological Association—with the largest number of votes in the association's history, as he likes to emphasize himself. At around this time he, too, had his epiphany. He was mowing the lawn while his daughter, Nicky, who had just turned five years old, was playing in the grass. Seligman, despite having a large family of seven children, was not particularly fond of children. He sent his daughter away because he was too "time-urgent" and "task-oriented" (which I would translate here, somewhat freely and from my own experience, as "impatient" and "easily irritated"). She returned and explained to her father that since her fifth birthday she had not complained about anything. Before that she had been a "whiner," but no longer. It had been very hard to change that. Had he noticed? Of course, said Seligman. "Daddy," said Nicky, "If I can manage to stop whining, you can also manage to stop grumbling." Seligman realized in that moment not only that he had been a grumbler for fifty years; he changed his attitude in the long term and now saw things more positively. And he also recognized in that moment that bringing up children was not just a question of correcting mistakes, but more so of encouraging their strengths. And finally, he realized that he must put an end to his research into victims, suffering, and trauma in the social sciences. He had had enough of making unhappy people less unhappy. Now he would devote his attention to the really big questions in life: What makes life worth living? What is happiness? What are values? What is meaningfulness? What are strengths?

Seligman had become famous through his research into the behavior of dogs. He subjected them to electric shocks: one group could "save" itself by pressing a lever, while the other group was subjected to the shocks without any means of help. In the following experiments they endured this torture passively although they, like the control group, would have had a chance to escape. Seligman found this "learned helplessness" in humans too. In his experiments only five out of eight were actually helpless, but about one third of each group defied the events, no matter how adverse they might be, and remained optimistic and healthy. About one in ten was helpless from the start, even without any intervention. Seligman thus confirmed the results of Antonovsky's questioning of women in the menopause, 29 percent of whom had remained mentally healthy and optimistic in spite of concentration camp and the experience of war. (As we shall see, approximately the same ratio of the workforce are attached emotionally to their work strongly, only slightly or not at all.)

Following his wake-up call, Seligman now wanted to focus his attention on the question of how "learned helplessness," or avoidance strategies, could be overcome. He began to study optimism. Like Antonovsky before him, he discovered that the people who did not become helpless were those who regarded life and its challenges as predictable and controllable through their own efforts. People with this feeling of coherence had a stronger immune system, were less depressive, and professionally more successful; they also lived longer and above all more happily.

Seligman succeeded with this paradigm change. He refocused his spotlight, away from mental illness and towards joy, happiness, *flow,* and a sense of purpose—but also towards responsibility, strengths, will, and character. A part of the research funds followed him and the new treatments which, despite all justified criticism, help to make many aspects of life happier, more productive, and more fulfilling.*

Martin Seligman distinguishes three forms of happiness: the pleasurable, the good, and the meaningful life, and he examines the extent to which they are accessible to pharmacological intervention (as a clinical psychologist he is interested above all in the "therapeutic" and medicinal perspective of Positive Psychology). There are countless interventions for pleasurable life, from gluttony to alcohol to drugs in the form of legal anti-depressives and illegal ecstasy. They all react with neuronal circuits and stimulate parts of the brain, and are "short cuts to happiness."

The second form of happiness, which Seligman calls "Eudaimonia," is *flow*, the phenomenon that his friend Csíkszentmihályi researched and described. *Flow* can be attained by developing our talents: by evolving them as

---

* At this point I should like to mention briefly the colleagues whom Martin Seligman won over for his movement. In addition to Csíkszentmihályi, these are especially Ed Diener at the University of Illinois in Urbana-Champaign, whose special area was "subjective well-being"; George Vaillant, who headed a project at Harvard which attempts to discover what makes university graduates successful; and last but not least Christopher Peterson of the University of Michigan, whom Seligman commissioned to produce a classification of strengths and virtues, and who set out to gather universal desirable character qualities throughout the world, and to evaluate and map them. This is the centerpiece of the Positive Psychology movement, and is to become the opposite of the classification of mental disorders (*Diagnostic and Statistical Manual of Mental Disorders*, abbreviated to DSM). Peterson's team agreed on six characteristics, so called *core virtues*, and twenty-eight *character strengths*, which exist in all cultures and which give life meaning. The six core virtues are knowledge, courage, humanity, fairness, moderation, and transcendance; the strengths include curiosity, learning, integrity, love, self-control, modesty, hope, and humor.

strengths and devoting ourselves to an activity for which we can make use of these strengths.*

Seligman describes *flow* by means of a story from his time as a student at Princeton, where there was a research assistant called Julian Jaynes. Jaynes had been given the task of feeding the South American lizards in the laboratory. But the lizards rejected everything that he offered them, from dead flies to papaya to Chinese take-away, and one creature after another starved to death. One day, Jaynes came back from lunch and tried to offer the lizards a ham sandwich, but as always they refused it. So he put the ham sandwich on the table and started to read the *New York Times*. At some point the first part of the newspaper ended up on the bread. "The lizard glanced at this configuration, rose up onto its hind legs, swaggered round the room, leapt onto the table, tore the *New York Times* in shreds and ate the ham sandwich. The moral is that lizards do not copulate and they do not eat without first showing off their strengths and virtues. They have to hunt, kill, tear to pieces, and stalk up. And although we are much more complex than lizards, we need to do that too. There is no short cut for us on the way to attaining *flow*. We have to focus on our best strengths in order to achieve Eudaimonia. So can there be a short cut, a pharmacology?" Seligman doubts it.

Seligman sees the third form of happiness as experiencing a sense of purpose in life by using one's strengths in the service of something one believes to be bigger than oneself.

---

* That is America: a dichotomy of diagnostics of happiness and madness is created with the help of billions of dollars. The mountain gyrates and brings forth a mouse. In Europe, the philosopher sits down at his desk, thinks, and writes a book, for example about logotherapy. Both paths lead to Rome and essentially come to the same conclusions.

"The Self is not a good place for meaningfulness, and the bigger the thing you devote yourself to, the more meaning your life will have ... There is no short cut here. That is what life is about. One day there will probably be a pharmacology of pleasure, and there may be a pharmacology of positive emotions in general, but it is unlikely that there will be an interesting pharmacology of *Flows*. And it is not possible that there will be a pharmacology of meaningfulness."

Seligman's merit lies without doubt in his untiring efforts on behalf of the idea of learned optimism, strength-oriented work, and the meaning of *flow experience*. With his books (which include the bestsellers *Learned Optimism* and *Authentic Happiness*), and also with the Positive Psychology Center, of which he is the director, Seligman helps people to recognize their strengths.* Knowledge of our own strengths is an important act of self-knowledge and of knowing the strengths of our colleagues in order to support them so that they can make use of them effectively in the fulfillment of their tasks. And it is the most important step towards successful personal development. And for that we should thank Seligman.**

Another important representative of Positive Psychology is the Gallup Institute, which has carried out opinion polls on economic, social, and political topics since the mid-1930s. It became famous for its predictions regarding the presidential elections in the United States. Since 2005, the *Gallup World*

---

* The website of the Positive Psychology Center (which also bears the title *Authentic Happiness*) states that it aims to introduce people to Positive Psychology through readings, videos, research reports, etc. The website provides more than 25 questionnaires regarding self-knowledge and it can be used free of charge.

**For those wishing to find out more about Martin Seligman, we recommend the website *edge.org/conversation/martin_seligman-eudaemonia-the-good-life*.

Polls have also been carried out, with surveys in 160 countries that cover 98 percent of the adult population and draw up global indices on law and order, food and living, institutions and infrastructure, well-being and talent migration (*Braingain*), and also commitment to the workplace. After the death of its founder, George Gallup, the concern was acquired by the psychologist Don Clifton, who restructured it as a firm of management consultants. Today Clifton's son Jim is the Chairman and CEO of the organization whose headquarters are in Washington, DC. The concern is owned by its 2,000 employees; it has over twenty branches in the United States. Although the *Gallup Polls* produce a negative contribution margin of $10 million every year, Gallup continues to carry them out, because they regularly hit the headlines and thus ensure the topicality of the concern. Today it is the Management Consultancy section of the concern that produces most of the revenues.

During the Second World War, Don Clifton was a pilot and gunman of a B-24 bomber. After being awarded the Distinquished Flying Cross, he decided that from then onward he wanted to devote himself to doing good for humanity. In the mid-1990s, long before Seligman's epiphany, he asked himself a simple question: "What would happen if we no longer asked what our employees were doing wrong, but only what they were doing right?"

Clifton began to study in the library of the University of Nebraska-Lincoln, and discovered once again that all the books on psychology were only concerned with what made people ill, and not what kept them healthy. Clifton wanted people to take full advantage of their potential, so that they not only "understand who they are, but also who they could become." He developed the *Clifton StrengthFinder* and presented his concept in his bestseller *Now, Discover Your Strengths* (the idea of the strengths test was developed by the late Chip Anderson, an Evangelical teacher in California). In 2003, shortly before his death, Clifton was honored for his work as the founder of Positive Psychology by the American Psychological Association.

In partnership with Marcus Buckingham and Curt Coffman, two further influential representatives of Positive Psychology, he developed *CliftonStrengths*—formerly the *Clifton Strengths-Finder*—and the *Employee Engagement Survey Q12* for Gallup. The latter served the Institute in particular as a starting point for the further commercialization of various consultancy services. In the meantime, Coffman offers his own *Employee Engagment Survey*.

A further pillar of the company is Gallup Press, the internal publishing department. The management bestseller *First, Break All the Rules: What the World's Greatest Managers Do Differently* by Marcus Buckingham and Curt Coffman was published here, as was the updated version of *StrengthsFinder 2.0*, titled *Now, Discover Your Strengths* as well as *How Full Is Your Bucket?*, edited by Gallup scientist Tom Rath and his grandfather, Don Clifton (it is tempting to say: *family business* of course).*

Buckingham and Coffman represent in essence the same principles as Fredmund Malik in his book *Managing Performing Living*. The difference is that Malik arrives at them from experience and thinking, while Gallup at least claims to

---

* It is not for nothing that Gallup is the subject of accusations of profiteering. In order to take the test and learn about 5 out of 34 personality constructs, you must purchase the book *Now, Discover Your Strengths*. The book explains the concept and also contains a voucher with a code which enables the reader to take the test on the Gallup website. If you want to see all 34 "strengths" it will cost $500, and if you want a complete interpretation of the test results it will cost $1,750.

have measured what successful companies and executives do differently (as summarized by Buckingham/Coffman). Both schools of thought emphasize correctly the importance of the orientation of goals, tasks, and strengths (it is always comforting that philosophical observation and empirical science arrive at the same result).

According to the Gallup Institute, since 1999 more than twenty-two million people have taken the *CliftonStrengths* test, and over ninety percent of the Fortune 500 companies use the test to teach their executives and their teams strengths-oriented employee development. The test follows the model of Positive Psychology and includes thirty-four subjects of the likes of "Doing," "Influencing," "Social Competence," and "Strategic Thinking," in 180 questions. If we are to believe Gallup's information, the test helps to recognize more clearly one's own gifts and those of others.

All strengths have so-called "balconies" and "basements," that is, the "balcony" of a strength that has been correctly and effectively employed, and the "basement" in which it is overstretched. For example, the strengths of curiosity and thirst for knowledge can lead to the fact that one is always up to date in one's chosen specialist area (balcony), or also to frittering one's time hopelessly away and losing sight of the goal (basement). Discipline can become obsessive perfectionism. Self-confidence can lead to hubris and arrogance. Ambition to greed. Imagination to eccentricity. Harmony to permissiveness. Assertiveness to tyranny, and caution to risk-aversion, etc. The more we succumb to self-reflection and focus on our strengths, and the less we confront the concrete task in its context, the greater is the danger of self-deception. We cannot determine ourselves whether a talent is of value, in other words how competent and competitive we are; that will be defined in the big wide world. A test which does not objectivize the subjective self-perception through a normative external assessment, is deceptive and largely useless for the selection of employees, and for many other applications in staff development it is questionable at the least.

Weaknesses should not be a taboo subject in human resources work: unfortunately, it does happen that human resources departments abuse the strengths-based approach to whitewash and placate in situations where there are no extenuating circumstances. Then the subject of weaknesses is abolished, and the very word itself may not be mentioned; weaknesses become challenges, development opportunities or even "minor" strengths. This may perhaps represent a congenial corollary for those who are notoriously conflict-averse; it is not, however, a sensible strategy for conflict avoidance, because it means that the potentially successful development instruments "strengthening strengths" are caricatured and do not enable us to measure ourselves within the world, but focus exclusively on the self-preoccupation propagated in thousands of self-help books on positive thinking: self-fulfillment in the form of self-discovery, self-development, and self-pampering as antipodes to the self-forgetfulness which is necessary in the search for meaning.

The Positive Psychology, with which Martin Seligman and Gallup are inseparably linked, has been the subject of a wide range of criticism today. However, the most fundamental criticism and at the same time the most important suggestions come from the disciples of Viktor Frankl. In the face of increasing evidence of the decisive role of meaningfulness for well-being and healing, they demand more sense-oriented studies. It remains to be seen what shape these might take and whether Positive Psychology will even respond to this suggestion.

When I asked Seligman about the fact that his publications and Positive Psychology websites ignore Frankl's work, he answered as follows: "Dear Volker, well, that is strange, because I regularly teach on the subject of Viktor Frankl. In fact, this weekend I have just given my class his book [referring to *Man's Search for Meaning*] to read. When I get the opportunity I shall check through my quotes to see whether in fact I really have not quoted him, although his work on meaning is so significant. All the best, Martin."

It would indeed be of great benefit if Seligman were able to make the movement he founded more balanced. In other words, to include not only activities, but also suffering and death as vital and meaningful experiences, to allow for less laboratory and more reality, to think less in a scientific-reductionist way and more holistically and humanistic-existentially. To put it simply, to combine the best of American empiricism and European dialectics. It would help the movement to new pluralistic modesty. With interventions directed towards meaningfulness, we could help to realize our longing for meaningfulness and self-transcendance. Let us hope that the Positive Psychology movement, complemented by the knowledge derived from the philosophy of Viktor Frankl, will catch on in the next decades in both Europe and the United States. Because simply considering the principles of Viktor Frankl would advance Positive Psychology considerably.

How the concern and employees at Red Bull achieve a meaningful approach to working together

// Essentially, talent is personality in the right place. //
TOMAS CHAMORRO-PREMUZIC

Everyone knows what they do not like doing. What robs them of energy. They are the things we avoid or we carry out quickly and reluctantly. You might think that only masochists would choose an occupation which consists primarily of such activities. Unfortunately, most employees follow this recipe for unhappiness. As already mentioned, the *Gallup Engagement Index* (carried out among millions of employees) regularly proves that only about fifteen percent experience a strong emotional bond with their work; seventy percent have only a slight connection, and another fifteen percent no bond at all. The results vary from year to year and from country to country, but the basic conclusion remains the same: Statistically speaking, only two out of ten employees are committed to the company and their work; and at least one has already resigned mentally or is working against the company, while seventy percent are working to rule. If you then subtract the employees who are currently only part of the onboarding process, it becomes clear how much potential is lying idle. In soccer, the situation would be as follows: Of the eleven players on the field, only three are playing with full commitment, but one of them is only under 16 and therefore only counts as a half in the team; seven of them are passing the ball listlessly back and forth in the defense area; and one of them has been bribed by the betting mafia and is playing for the opposing team. However, since the position in the opposing team is similar, the game ends in a draw. If there were any spectators, they would leave the stadium immediately and never return. It would be a declaration of bankruptcy and the end of soccer as a sport.

There are a number of factors which can further strengthen this situation of detachment in a company: the uncertainties of the labor market, fear of change and—albeit only occasionally—overpayment. But also framework conditions relating to labor politics can demotivate: for example, in countries with strict employment protection, the *Engagement Level* will be even lower than elsewhere. We should encourage people who are not committed and who no longer work *for a* company, but merely *in a* company, to change their lives and seek new challenges. The legal framework conditions should support this. And yet, the opposite is the case: severance indemnities and pension claims, which are relinquished if an employee resigns, together with exaggerated employment protection, are often reasons why people fail to do so.

What would happen if seven out of ten employees were motivated? There would be an explosion of productivity and innovation. Turnover and profits would rise noticeably, and fluctuation rates would fall. The gains from taxes and business results could be invested in talent promotion and increased flexibility. There would be a revolution in the management of knowledge work.

In order to get closer to achieving this utopia, companies and employees must think together about how we can work with a focus on meaningfulness in a project. As we know, talent is personality in the right place, as the psychologist Tomas Chamorro-Premuzic has aptly put it. So the central question is: Where do the unique talents of the employees lie, and where is the right place to make use of them effectively for the company? If we are to believe Gallup, companies which encourage a strength-oriented development have more committed employees and therefore considerably less fluctuation, considerably higher performance and therefore, as can be expected, a higher turnover and bigger profits. People with confidence in their strengths are noticeably happier, experience *flow* more frequently, progress more rapidly up the career ladder, and remain longer in their job.

When I now describe more specifically below a synergy of this nature between company and employees towards meaningful work, then my assessments refer in all cases to my experiences from the day-to-day corporate routine at Red Bull. However, since Red Bull has always cultivated a management approach focused towards meaningfulness—and is appreciated by its staff (and also by potential applicants) for precisely this—the following can easily be translated as a general recommendation, albeit admittedly with a personal accent.

Let us start with the staff. What are the decisive steps, both before applying and then upon joining a company? It is always surprising to note that many people are not really aware of their talents, strengths, and weaknesses, and hence have no idea what exactly they want to do. They do not apply for a task, but rather for a position within a company. Understandably, attractive employers are very popular among applicants. An *Employer Value Proposition* of this kind, EVP for short, depends to a large extent on the factors market share, innovative ability, and productivity of a company. A high *EVP* equates with many applicants for a small number of jobs. The survey among more than 10,000 students at thirty-four universities in Austria shows that Red Bull is regularly the most popular employer amongst students. That is gratifying for Red Bull and shows that, according to the students, the company offers good future prospects. Red Bull is the world market leader in its business areas, and within its sector it is the epitome of innovation, which is why we can only concur with the students. As an employee, you will find a good environment in general and, statistically speaking, you will also have better promotional possibilities.

The bad news is that only very few graduates will have the chance to work for a top concern. Red Bull Austria receives some 8,000 applications every quarter. Only a very small number of applicants will have a chance to be offered one of the coveted jobs. (The good news is that the task is much more important than the company, and there is more than one good company in each sector that will offer a sound working environment).

Of the 8,000 applicants to Red Bull, many of them simply want to "work for a cool company," and the job is "a minor consideration," in line with the motto, "I'll do anything, as long as Red Bull is on my business card and they give me a company car." However, the candidates should ask themselves whether they expect the work to be meaningful for them and to give them pleasure; whether they will be equal to the task; and whether they will be able to make use of their strengths. It is not the position that is of prime importance, but rather the tasks associated with the position that will decide whether they can make use of their gifts. So from the beginning it is the task that should be in the foreground, not the company, the position, the money, or the career. I personally always find applicants who think less about the salary, the position, and the negotiations, but who ask more questions concerning the employer's expectations and their specific activities in their day-to-day work, refreshing.

Ideally, the choice of occupation will be a systematic continuation of the fostering of talent that takes place at school and university. The greater the degree of specialization during education, the more limited the professional options will be. Those who know what their talent is can choose the specialization at an early stage. Those who are not sure will be well advised to follow a broader range of options. This may sound trivial, but the prerequisite for the decision regarding an independent choice of profession is that one should make the choice as far as possible independently of the ideas of the outside world. Regardless of the corresponding inclinations, you should not decide on a profession only because that is what your parents do, or because there is a family firm, or perhaps because there is a training place in the vicinity where there is a vacancy. And the career prospects within a sector can change and should not serve as the sole means of orientation.

Furthermore, you should have completed a course of training before joining a company. The transition from being a student to the world of work is a major change which will be easier if there is a clear distinction between the two phases of life. The eternal student, who has a part-time job on the side, is a symbol for this unresolved transition.

Equally as important as the first choice of profession is also the possibility of trying out during one's early years what one enjoys doing and how one can develop one's talents into real strengths. The more varied the job, and the more you are able to try out, the better. In the age of knowledge work, life is a constant learning process. During each change of job, sometimes only when taking up a new position, we should ask ourselves whether our talents are in the right place. My recommendation would be periodically, for example at the beginning of every year, to question what must be done for the good of the company and which contribution you personally, or you with your department, can make. "Which activities am I good at personally? Which ones can I delegate or pass on to people who can do them better than I can? Not only *where*, but above all *why* am I successful or unsuccessful?" We should keep an eye on all that when choosing a profession, when applying for a position, or when planning our annual goals.

Many employees, however, have only a limited range of tasks to accomplish. If it is not possible to change these, we shall need to change ourselves and our attitude. Martin Seligman tells the story of a "bagger" at Genuardi's, a chain of department stores which has been taken over by Safeway in the meantime. In America a "bagger" is someone who packs the customer's purchases into bags after they have been paid for. We evidently have no need of this valuable service in Europe. This bagger did not have a particularly high opinion of her job, which she probably found too monotonous. In any case, she took Seligman's test, and it transpired that her principal strength lay in her social intelligence. From that point onward she regarded her job of packing the food into bags as an opportunity to start a conversation with the customers. The packing was a side issue and the conversation with the customers was an interesting way of passing the time. Her job, which she had previously found boring, became predominantly a *flow experience*, during which the time really flew by.*

Let us turn now to the company's contribution. Companies which make use of the strengths and weaknesses of people will make sure that positive thinking, the feeling of being able to make a difference, commitment to a task, and links with other people are given priority, together with meaningfulness through a valuable contribution to the whole.

Let us remember: meaningfulness means to apply our energies to something. As a question of conscience, meaningfulness contains a personal value judgment, which is why meaning cannot simply be prescribed or conjured up by means of incentives. Meaningfulness as a prerequisite for sustainable motivation cannot be prescribed collectively, but can only be found personally. But we should remember that meaningfulness can vary depending upon the stage of our lives in which we find ourselves. It will generally be defined differently by someone embarking on their professional life from that of an executive with ten years of professional experience and a family, and quite differently again by someone who is on the verge of retirement. No organization can convey a sense of meaningfulness over the course of time to all employees with their different life plans and biographies. So there is no meaningful organization, only meaningful tasks. Those who make a good choice here will enjoy their work, work longer, and perform better.

---

* Buckingham and Coffman supply in *First, Break All The Rules* numerous other striking examples in which top achievements were produced by employees in very mundane jobs, because they applied their talents and strengths in the right place within the company, whether they were truck drivers, cleaners, or sales staff.

However, each of us must find their own task. In almost thirty years I rarely experienced a situation in which Mateschitz would ask someone if they wanted to take over a task. Once I was the person he asked. It was in the mid-2000s, when Mateschitz almost casually and on the sidelines of negotiations relating to Formula One in London, and once again in a taxi, asked me if I would like to become his assistant. At that stage I was not aware of the implicit consequences of the question. My task at that time was to build up a Human Resources department, and I was kept very busy as the head of the legal department. I told him so, and that was an end of the matter. I did not regret my decision. It was the right one.

Red Bull focused its Human Resources work systematically towards meaningfulness and strength orientation. Each employee is recommended to take a strengths test for his or her development. *Strength Workshops* are offered individually or within the framework of the two-day staff training program, the *People Management Program*, or PMP for short. Every two years we measure the *commitment* in the departments with our specially developed My Experience Engagement Tool. In this way, the contribution of the manager and also that of the staff, in the sense of personal responsibility as described by Frankl, are measured via the dimensions "meaning," "freedom and responsibility," "strength orientation," and "relationship orientation."

The *commitment* of an organization allows us to make very accurate conclusions about the management and future fluctuation rates. This is valuable information for the corporate management. Fluctuation rates of thirty percent and more mean, for example, that during every fourth year you will be dealing with a completely new work force, at least statistically speaking. Exit questioning, including a net promoter score, is also important, as are statements on the extent to which employees leaving the company would recommend the organization. The Engagement Survey is carried out anonymously every year. The employees receive the results even before their superior and discuss them and give feedback.

Knowledge about the strengths of the staff and their annual feedback help to find the right tasks for them, and in practice this protects from the danger of succumbing to the rhetorical question as to why the employee is not as perfect as was expected or hoped for. The solution to the conundrum is at hand: perhaps his talents lie elsewhere. To encourage talents and strengths in the context of the tasks is the "esteem" which Frankl referred to when he said you should regard people as what they could be. It is the opposite of the reductionist search for staff through competence profiles, which will be obsolete when people with talents join the company. Recognizing talents and developing them into strengths will become an important development tool.

As already mentioned, Red Bull receives thousands of applications every day. Worldwide they amount to almost half a million every year, for possibly 5,000 job vacancies. So the company is right at the front in the famous "war of talent." However, the search for the right talents for the small number of jobs resembles the proverbial search for the needle in the haystack. And then the applicants are also our consumers. Those who take the trouble to apply for a job at Red Bull are usually not just looking for a job; they identify with the world of Red Bull and want to become part of it. So we not only have a responsibility towards our applicants as potential employers, but they are also predominantly users of the product and as such are brand-savvy. Dietrich Mateschitz therefore placed great emphasis at the outset on ensuring that each applicant received a personal answer. Originally he wrote those answers himself, but then passed the task on to a staff consultancy; today it is the task of the Human Resources department at Red Bull. But how can you reply personally to half a million applicants per year?

By giving them something back. And what could suggest itself more obviously than to support applicants in getting to know themselves better? For this we use the *Red Bull Wingfinder*. This is a strengths-based test which is free of charge and which helps all our applicants to assess their talents and abilities better. In contrast to the *Clifton Strength-Finder*, which takes into account only the subjective results of their own questionnaire, but not those of the other participants, and which therefore fails as a development and selection criterion because of the absence of a normative examination, the Red Bull Wingfinder permits statements regarding the objective suitability as a knowledge worker. It is our way of saying thank you for the application to Red Bull. For cost reasons, tests of this kind usually come only at the end of the application process and only for a small number of potential candidates. It helps us to assess the strengths of a large number of applicants more accurately at the very beginning of the application process, and to decide whether the person concerned is suitable for a specific post at Red Bull. The *Wingfinder* therefore provides not only strength feedback but also serves as a selection tool.

The test was developed by Red Bull and a team of experts who were professors of psychology, especially Dr. Tomas Chamorro-Premuzic, Professor of Business Psychology at

University College London and Columbia University and Chief Innovation Officer at Manpower. The Red Bull Wingfinder is based on thirty years of research in psychology, carried out in thousands of scientific studies and analyses. It takes into account one's own perception and relates it to external benchmarks. This enables reliable statements where the applicant being tested is compared with a normative peer group.* The Red Bull Wingfinder is intuitively designed and makes use wherever possible of visual questions, with the result that over ninety percent of the participants who begin the test will also complete it.

There is a consensus in business psychology that there are three areas which have more influence on the career success of a knowledge worker than others. "What are the main ingredients of talent? Although there are millions of jobs, people who are more intelligent, better motivated, and more curious, and who get on with others, will do better in every job. Based on this robust talent model and an ultra-modern scientific method, the Red Bull Wingfinder is an unparalleled attempt to help millions of people to identify and develop their career potential," writes Chamorro-Premuzic. The Wingfinder provides information about the so-called "RAW components" relating to talents: *rewarding to deal with* (social skills), *able to do the job* (a skill or intelligence that corresponds to the demands made by the position), and *willing to do the job* (drive and motivation). The Red Bull Wingfinder includes a total of 25 strengths in the areas of social competence, fluid intelligence, creativity, and willingness to perform. It tests these within the space of thirty-five

---

* The test was subjected to a rigorous validation which is presented and explained in detail on *wingfinder.com*.

minutes by means of 280 questions in five different assessment formats. Applicants are measured against themselves and against others. The assessment provides participants not only with valuable insight into their strengths; it also gives them coaching instructions for measures and development in their working lives.

Currently, some 250,000 people make use of the offer in seven languages under *wingfinder.com* every year. And counting. Various partners help Red Bull to make it even better known.

The recognition of strengths and making the right use of them within the company is one thing. Equally important, however, is who one reports to, who the line superior is. And here, despite all the planning and thought, sometimes this also includes an element of luck. There are true *Talent Champions*—people who as managers devote an extra hour, statistically speaking, to their staff every day. These are the "natural" leaders, who know that it takes clear goals, who recognize talents and strengths, and who encourage above all trusting cooperation.

The prerequisite for the latter is also predictability. For successful relationships and the development of individual potential in a company, you need—as in a family home, incidentally—clear goals and agreements and predictable and consistent reactions to deviations from the pursuit of goals. Moreover, individualization is important: Management consists primarily of the recognition of the uniqueness of employees. A good manager treats each employee differently, knows their strengths and weaknesses, supports, demands, encourages, understands, forgives, and finds the right positions and tasks in line with that individual's strengths.* He will individualize salary, motivation, and even the car as far as possible. As a good manager, he will fight against the leveling down practiced by the staff council and the administration. The staff council wants to see everyone equally well treated in a collective manner, and the staff administration aims to see them all managed with equal efficiency in a utilitarian manner. Those whose leader resists this can count themselves lucky, and should not make the mistake of thinking that is a matter of course. And those who do not report to a "talent champion" should remember: In spite of everything, self-knowledge, modesty, and performance-oriented work remain the gateway to success. The less you overestimate yourself, the easier it is for colleagues to see you as what you could be. The less we expect and the more we contribute, the more welcome we shall be in the team. Even with "normal" superiors and colleagues.

The three most important decisions made by a manager when dealing with colleagues are, firstly: who to employ; secondly, who to promote; and thirdly, what salary to pay whom. These decisions must be taken conscientiously, in such a way that they will stand up to your conscience. There must be no cliques, no politics, and no favors. And the decisions must be made autonomously and subjected to a judgment which is based solely on the facts. The more the company influences this decision, the more control the

---

* Jürgen Klopp, for example, is considered to be brilliant in the recognition of individual character. The football professional Kevin-Prince Boateng described him in the SPIEGEL interview of April 18, 2020 as follows: "You have to understand the players, you can't simply hit out; you have to know how they tick. Klopp knows that for each of his players; he knows how he has to deal with them: You, come here, you're crazy, bang bang. And he's put his arms round another one, cuddle him. That's what I mean."

manager will lose. And this can lead to an absolute loss of control. When the employee is allocated, the Human Resources department calculates the salary rise, and the committee for succession planning determines which member of the team will be promoted. In this case the manager will know that he is not the leader of the travel group, but only the tour guide.

As the head of Human Resources, I repeatedly receive phone calls as to whether I could put in a good word for an applicant, usually the son or daughter of the caller. I always ask whether the caller could imagine not being able to choose the members of his or her team personally, but that they were simply allocated to the team. Imagining this situation makes the intervention appear what it actually is: absurd. Nonetheless, there must be companies that employ staff in this way, otherwise I would not receive so many calls of this nature. That doesn't mean that a four-week internship which is granted to do a partner, supplier, or a customer a favor, will destroy the corporate culture. The filling of important positions, however, must take place without the interference of politics and relationships, and exclusively in accordance with objective criteria, in other words in line with the requirements of the position and on the basis of the talent and experience of the applicant.

The business partners in the Human Resources department assist the manager in defining precisely the assignments, and when possible in finding an acceptable number of suitable applicants. The final choice of the employee, and hence the responsibility, will lie, however, solely with the hiring manager. If he or she is to assume responsibility for the team, he must also be in the position to assemble it. This principle should apply not only to companies, but to all organizations, especially also in the public sector, for example in schools. Because the most important task of a manager will be to find the right people for the right tasks.

A good education is the basic requirement for success in professional life. Primary schools teach the cultural skills, and vocational schools and universities prepare the young person for his or her career. Moreover, the learning of a talent-oriented personal working method in school and as a student is more useful than blindly accumulating knowledge. The cultural skills of reading, writing, and arithmetic—and increasingly the mastery of information technologies—are the exclusion criteria in the knowledge professions. Those who do not reach an acceptable level in these basic skills will always be at a disadvantage in the knowledge professions. The "tools" of the knowledge professions, including reporting, budget preparation, descriptions of tasks and positions, the setting of targets, control, and performance assessment build on these basic skills. They can be assessed with an aptitude test. An exclusion criterion will be if the candidate lies in the bottom third of the comparison group; in other words, if more than two thirds of the persons being tested produced better results in these central basic skills. That is to say: an aptitude test can help with the assessment as to whether a candidate's skills mean they are the right person for a position, but it is in fact far better suited to show that the candidate is not suitable. A candidate who does not possess an acceptable level of cultural skills will show this in the test. That saves the company and also the applicant time and money, which is always better than discovering, three months after the employee joins the financial accounting department, that he or she cannot add up accurately. If an applicant is not able to fulfill the basic tasks of the job either verbally or numerically after receiving appropriate training, it would be better to look for another occupation, possibly as an artisan—and that is not intended to be disparaging in any way. To make use of a clichéd image: a fulfilled life as a talented joiner is more worthwhile in every way than being a frustrated academic reduced to driving a taxi.

The task facing every manager and the Human Resources department at Red Bull is to "find the right people, realize their talents, and keep them." A good application process requires time and patience, however. It is a lack of time that frequently impairs the quality of the selection process. Accordingly, the hiring manager should insist that job interviews are only carried out with those candidates who are basically suitable for the vacancy. The suitability test will help here. In addition, there should be a precise job description which defines the tasks which will probably have to be completed during the next one to two years. Only then can you know which candidate profile will be required. The board of the Vienna Philharmonic will need to know when looking to fill the post of conductor, whether they will be required to lead a performance of *The Magic Flute* or *Kontinent Rihm*. And the choice of candidate will be made accordingly.

Ideally, you will have a suitable candidate on your 'virtual substitute bench', a potential employee you know from previous activities, from negotiations, or from lectures and seminars. If this is not the case, the post will be advertised or you will commission a headhunter. Almost without exception, however, neither the Human Resources department nor the headhunter will find an employee, but will produce only more or less suitable candidates.

Depending on the case in question, the manager should insist on a minimum of between two and five suitable candidates. He will be the one to make the choice. Only he knows the precise tasks. And it is his responsibility. The new employee will become his colleague, not that of the headhunter or the Human Resources department. Good Human Resources staff will provide the manager with an informative CV for each candidate, and will have already clarified the main points of their career. The certificate of good conduct and the suitability test were both satisfactory, so the applicant has not been excluded.

The next stage will be the job interview. To put it crudely, there are good and bad conversations. In bad conversations, the applicant may hardly say a word (and the manager holds forth about the job, the great company, its culture, and about himself), or being a member of the same soccer club proves to be the decisive reason for employment. In good conversations, on the other hand, it will be a question of drawing up a prognosis for the future on the basis of past experiences and, hopefully, also successes.

A good job interview takes time. We should not shy away from running through everything from A to Z, from education to winning the lottery. Each position the candidate has held should be understood as a whole. What were the associated tasks? What were the main successes and failures of this part of his or her career? Who was the boss concerned? What is the candidate particularly proud of, and what is he ashamed of to this day? I like to remind the applicant that his statements regarding the position in question will be checked by asking his superior for a reference (this method is known as the *Threat of a Reference Check*, or *TORC* for short).* What will the superior say with regard to the strengths and weaknesses of the applicant? Were they in charge of other employees? If yes, how many? What exactly did these other employees do, and what did the applicant do? How would they describe the applicant and his management style?

Even more important than the question of where the applicant's successes lie, is the question of why this was so. For example, that might be the waiter's ability to convince the guest, or the nurse's skill in knowing how the patient must be feeling, or the salesman's ability to be persistent. If I am curious and ask the applicants why they are successful and effective managers, I may perhaps recognize that they have the ability to individualize. An experienced and good manager listens precisely and looks for patterns, the famous "golden thread." Which specific activities does the applicant find easy? Why does the candidate want this position? What exactly does he or she imagine they will do? Ultimately, this is the search for the Holy Grail, the tracking down of talent, strengths, and *flow*. I therefore also like to ask about happiness and contentment. When were you happy in your life? What would you change if you had the chance to do so?

When the conversation appears to have come to an end and the applicant has already relaxed and is about to leave the room, I always ask three more questions which allow me to draw conclusions concerning the applicant's talents. The first question is about the past: Does the candidate remember a situation during his or her past, when time flew

---

* See Bradford D. Smart, *Topgrading: The Proven Hiring and Promoting Method That Turbocharges Company Performance*, New York 2012.

past and he or she was completely absorbed in what they were doing? In short: When did they experience a sort of *flow* for the first time while doing something?

Once the surprise at this unexpected question has died down, I usually get to hear an answer referring to various children's games. Building sandcastles, a puppet play, playing with the children from the neighborhood in the nearby woods—the answers tell me more about the candidate's talents than they realize. Did the *flow* occur during an activity alone or with others? Was the main emphasis on patience, stamina, or logical thinking? When playing with other children, was being present or winning important? Let us remind ourselves: concentration on a game at an early age allows us to guess that the child was following its talents.

The second question focuses on the future. The candidate is asked to imagine exactly what he or she would do if they were to win seventy million euros in the lottery. The answers are sometimes astounding and reveal the secret wishes of many candidates. Not only that; at the same time, they show us a great deal about our unused talent potential. For example, I had one candidate who said that he was contented and happy. So, he could have chosen to carry on as before, use the millions to buy himself a dream house and then distribute the rest among his family and his bank account. Instead, he said at the interview that he would spend it on traveling to exotic countries in order to perfect his talent as a nature photographer. I asked him what was preventing him from doing that here and now? Money should play only a subsidiary role.

And the third question I like to ask is the conundrum devised by Daniel Kahneman concerning the cost of a tennis ball and racket, which he describes in his bestseller *Thinking, Fast and Slow*. Kahneman is the only psychologist to have won the Nobel Prize for Economics, and one of the few Nobel prizewinners outside the Chicago School. He knows about the inadequacies of human judgment as well as the model of the "invisible hand" which regulates everything on the markets and makes any form of state intervention unnecessary. He counters these assumptions concerning a functioning *Homo oeconomicus* far removed from reality in the world of neo-liberalism with his conviction which "on the one hand guarantees personal freedom and on the other brings people to make decisions they will not regret at a later date." In his bestseller, he explains the susceptibility to error of human thought processes. In numerous experiments he demonstrates that our brain likes to switch onto auto-pilot, which ultimately optimizes the energy consumption of the brain and hence contributes to our survival. Only a few of us can change tack quickly in critical situations and think through the task carefully. The others are deceived in Kahneman's brain-teasers by the apparently obvious.

The question about the cost of the tennis ball and racket is just one such example: A tennis racket and a ball together cost €1.10. The racket costs one euro more than the ball. How much does the racket cost, and how much does the ball cost? Try it! You will find the answer below. And take comfort from the fact that even most Harvard graduates did not answer correctly.*

A job interview with a candidate who has experience and who has already held a number of positions (which could also have been in the same company), can thus last

---

* Wrong answer: Racket 1 euro, ball 10 cents. Correct answer: Racket 1 euro and 5 cents, ball 5 cents.

for two hours or more. If you take this amount of time, both people involved, the applicant and the manager, will be rewarded with valuable insights into the expected tasks within the company and the personality of the applicant. There is a good chance that the right employee will be entrusted with the right tasks in the right position. For the employee, this could mean long-term success and fulfillment, and for the executive and his or her effectiveness, the avoidance of the effort, costs, and frustration, which inevitably result from appointing the wrong person.

Once the conversations are over, if the result is a positive one, the contract negotiations will follow. Here, too, there are aspects to bear in mind which will point to the suitability of employees, especially executives. If someone has no comments to make about the draft contract, this indicates that they work superficially and are possibly inclined to turn a blind eye to certain details. And, conversely, I have also experienced that literally every comma is questioned. For me, that is a critical hint that someone could be self-centered and over-correct, and hence unsuitable to be a manager. Now, the reader may object that it is hardly possible to generalize about such qualities during contract negotiations. My experience based on contract negotiations with candidates and their further track record at Red Bull allows me to suspect at least that such details should be taken into account, in order to arrive at a final judgment as to whether an applicant will probably fail to fulfill the expected tasks or will be successful.

And so we come to a further important decision of every executive, namely, the question as to who should be promoted. Ideally, in fact, the recruiting should not take place externally, but the manager should have a suitable candidate to fill an open or newly created vacancy in his or her team.

When promoting staff, managers should take "hungry" colleagues into account, those who want to carve out a career for themselves and assume responsibility. When deciding on the promotion, it is important to take care that no one is forced into a manager role in line with the so-called Peter Principle: that they are promoted to their own level of incompetence. As we at Red Bull unfortunately had to discover with some well-intended promotions, an assistant, even if (or precisely because) they achieve an outstanding performance, is only very rarely a suitable candidate to take on the position of their superior when this becomes available. It is also important to remember that not only management, but also expertise is responsible for the success of a company. Real knowledge workers are experts in their field and will drive innovation. In the best case they are also good managers, but if not, as long as position and budget allow it, they should have someone at their side who is. Management tends to be undervalued at Red Bull, too. Whenever absolute top performances are achieved, the exceptionally skilled players are the top performers, and managers secure the success in the background. Adrian Newey and Christian Horner, Head of Red Bull Racing, as well as Ralf Rangnick and Oliver Mintzlaff (former managing director of RB Leipzig and today one of three managing directors of Red Bull, responsible for international projects) are good examples of how expertise and management can complement each other.

Please allow me at this point a few words on the subject of meaningfulness in what is known as "succession planning" in a company. In my experience, promotions cannot be planned systematically with a reasonable amount of effort. The lists of supposedly suitable candidates to take over all posts, or certain key positions within the company, drawn up with considerable effort, turn out in most cases not to be very meaningful. The fact that executives have great difficulty agreeing on a list of high potentials, lies in the nature of succession planning: static lists do not provide a solution to dynamic challenges. A good manager does not *plan* the succession selectively in shorter or longer time intervals, but *prepares* suitable employees permanently for possible promotion.

Whether the successor to a specific post is successful or not, depends on whether a suitable candidate for the specific task can be found at the time that the position becomes available. These tasks are time-critical and can therefore hardly be adequately planned. And so it is not so much a question of the static position to be filled; what is far more important is the dynamic task which will be subject to an uncertain future which cannot be planned, and which the successor will have to overcome successfully. Only the manager can decide who is a suitable candidate at the time when the position becomes vacant. If a company is searching for a managing director, it will make a difference whether he aims to develop his market leadership in calm waters, or whether a competitor will force the company to reinvent itself. Whether a candidate really is suitable at the time when the vacant post needs to be filled, can indeed be prophesied in advance from your desk, but the effort it will take is out of all proportion.

Moreover, succession planning has the potential to demotivate a large section of the workforce. Within a company, nothing remains a secret permanently. That applies to succession planning too, which after all really is top secret. Generally, you will not be doing the "princes" who have been chosen as successors a favor. For the potential successor, this distinction hardly makes his or her work easier when dealing with colleagues, because the rest of the team will be bewildered. Some colleagues may wonder why they have not been chosen as the "prince." Envy, resentment, and a search for what they have done wrong will be the consequence. They will want to show the boss that he has made the wrong choice. And often the "prince" may even have already left the "kingdom" at the point when he is about to be "proclaimed king."

It is therefore not surprising that succession politics feature more frequently than succession planning during the time-consuming discussions by executives concerning succession planning. It is gratifying to see that companies increasingly see succession planning as what it actually is: a waste of time that can no longer be justified on the executive floors and in the Human Resources departments of companies.

What we can do, and ultimately must do, is to prepare our staff for the next task. Management is staff development through preparation for new tasks within the organization. Red Bull does precisely this with its succession preparation program.

In order to make this preparation a rewarding business for all concerned, the organization unit must be permitted to keep talent within its own ranks. Permanent institutionalized cross functional and cross organizational moves are career incentives that may easily be misunderstood. For heads of department and managing directors, it will become a frustrating Sisyphean task when they are permanently being robbed of the fruits of their labors in this field. They know best what the employee can or cannot do, in other words, which task will be best for him or her. This is the only way in which we can ensure the stability and sustainability that are so important in an organization. Nothing is more detrimental to success than constantly changing managers. They tend to neglect the HR work and staff development and to run the company by means of key data only. That leads to an optimization of results but also to a brain drain. Only a manager who remains in charge in the long term has a sustained interest in a strong team. And such teams do not deserve to permanently have new superiors put in front of them.

There are only two legitimate exceptions to this rule. Firstly, if a good employee is in danger of resigning because he wants to develop his career and there is no suitable position or task available for him within the organizational unit. Before this employee leaves the company and becomes a regretted loss who perhaps even moves over to the competition, the executive responsible should release him to another unit within the organization. If the executive in charge retains control over promotions and lateral moves of employees within the units of the organization, the bad habit of getting an incompetent employee moved to another department will automatically disappear.

On the other hand, as I have already mentioned, it should be possible for young employees to try themselves out and to try out as many different things as possible. In the first years after training they must have a playing field which will help them to discover their talents and strengths. Just as important as the first choice of occupation is therefore also the opportunity to try out where one's inclinations lie. The more varied the job, the better. Executives and companies should support this through various job assignments and—if possible—also job rotations. However, this process should have been completed by the age of thirty years, or thirty-five at the latest, and the employees should have found a fulfilling task as manager or expert. After all, this is the age at which our performance capacity is at its highest. Generally, it will be the next ten to fifteen years which will decide whether we will make it to the top or not. From the age of fifty, when our own performance capacity slowly starts to ebb, the development of our staff should be more important to us than our own career.

The last important adjusting screw for any manager will be decisions about pay. Deciding who is to receive which salary increase and bonuses is the litmus test for autonomy in management. The person who delegates this decision is not a true manager. Salary decisions cannot be avoided. They will be made annually—and not more frequently—by the top executive.

Imagine that you run your department like a craftsperson's business. There the employer will pay his employees exactly the amount that he can afford on the one hand, and that he must pay them on the other, in order to ensure that his staff do not run away. He will pay his good people well, better than the others, and if necessary up to the very limit, because he will not want to lose them to his competitors. The limit will lie where he can no longer support such a high salary because he can no longer explain it to the other employees. That is really all it takes to reach good pay decisions.

In most companies, there are numerous avoidance strategies in order to chicken out of facing this responsibility. The collectivist approach, as I call it, is widely adopted; that is, not to differentiate and to treat all employees equally. This is misunderstood solidarity and in the long run it will mean that the company will lose its high-performing staff, because those who are unequal are being treated the same, and because the good employees will see this as a lack of appreciation. Another popular approach is to attach the blame to the company or the human resources department, in line with the motto: "I would have liked to give you more, but my budget won't allow me to do so." What should an employee think of a manager if he cannot prevail within the company, even when it comes to a question that is as important for him as how much he earns.

There are, however, confrontation strategies as well as avoidance strategies. Particularly unpleasant for a manager are wildly exaggerated salary proposals by his staff for their staff in turn, in other words the nearest reporting line after their direct reports. This can occur either out of ignorance or deliberately, in order to claim a better salary for themselves as employees; after all, it would not be appropriate for the level below to earn almost as much or even more than one earns oneself. In this case it is essential to discourage such attempts energetically by means of suitable control measures. "I can tell which way the wind is blowing," is the code word at Red Bull for this transparent tactic. One should either intervene, whereby there is a risk that one will become the villain of the piece ("I would have asked for more on your behalf"), or one accepts the suggestion and makes up for the wrong decision by compensating for the mistake on the direct employee level: then this particular employee will not be granted a pay increase until he has learned to think like a businessperson. This is also the reason Dietrich Mateschitz left the salary of one or the other of those reporting to him directly unchanged, until they had learned to take responsible salary decisions.

Responsibility within a company is also relinquished where pay increases are confused with bonus allocation. Here, too, appropriate control and counter-measures will be required. Corporate profits will be distributed proportionately to the owners for the provision of capital and as a risk premium. Employees, on the other hand, receive a generous but always market-compliant payment that takes into account their individual successes in fulfilling their tasks. Some managers support a participative approach, and also want to see their staff participating in the profits. That is absolutely legitimate, if an organization commits to this policy. However, if—as is the case with Red Bull—the company's philosophy is to pay salaries appropriate to the employees' performance that are in line with the market plus bonuses, this participative approach will not be appropriate. The employees do not participate in the loss if one should occur.

Moreover, Red Bull categorically rejects automatic bonus systems with the exception of individual sales commissions. Bonus decisions are always made individually and after an assessment of the employee's performance by the manager. This judgment includes all components, so that windfall profits or calamities for which the employee is not responsible can also be assessed. An employee's bonus should not be affected by exchange rates or other imponderables which he or she cannot influence.

Salary decisions should always be taken over the long term, for years if not for decades, and should always take into account the employee's probable career path. Salary discussions are never task-oriented, but always turn towards self-reflection, and are therefore best avoided if possible. Take your decisions well-prepared and abide by them; do not make any corrections as a result of employee interventions. News of such interventions will spread and encourage other employees to question your decision. Salary decisions are not taken by means of democratic discourse, but are a decision by the executive. An executive who thinks more about his employees' salaries than his own remuneration has really arrived.

Ultimately, however, all salary adjustments must take place in line with the budget, which is why they must be consolidated at organization and concern level. While the manager assesses his employees and makes plans independently, his decisions will be examined in the background by a small Compensation & Benefits department, and if necessary will be questioned critically. That will occur, however, in just a few hundred cases out of over 10,000 employees. Here, people will concentrate on so-called outliers, employees with exceptionally large salary or bonus increases. If they are justified, they will be accepted. The more rigid the system is and the guidelines tend towards inflationary adjustment, the more pressure will be exerted. This generally leads to the anticipation of salary increases during recruiting, and to increased costs within the company: employees are awarded higher salaries upon appointment, in order to cushion the pressure on salaries arising during the first years of their career in the company.

This further bottom-up approach in the planning of staff costs requires a careful balancing of interests between maximum freedom and responsibility for the manager, while maintaining the background control by C&B. In order to ensure that the salaries remain affordable, performance-related, and in line with the market, the budgets must be maintained and the entrepreneurial approach practiced in the salary philosophy throughout the company. These principles are largely internalized by the entire organization and the staff, and it is surprising how little control is actually required.

In conclusion, let us turn to a further decisive point in the interaction between company and employee: the feedback. In my view, performance assessments are very hard to objectivize. In order for them to be honest feedback, they must basically always be confidential and remain personal, and should not be included in the employee's personal file. As a general rule, transparency leads to positive distortion, to "gilded" judgments. Business partners repeatedly complain that staff who have to be dismissed receive good or even excellent performance assessments in the final period. That is human and understandable, when you bear in mind that the assessment is not confidential. And an executive who does not want to discourage his staff would be well advised to end the annual conversation with positive future prospects. In many cases, it therefore comes to schematic assessments, as in a certificate of service. They are of no value to the employee or the company, and are yet another way of wasting time within the company.*

The Human Resources departments of companies should stop measuring the number of pointless performance assessment sheets, and instead demand what the majority of employees wish for: continuous assessment in real time, and

---

* On the internet you can even find instructions for schematic performance assessments. You will find sixty *effective performance review phrases* under *cultureamp.com/blog/performance-review-phrases/*.

high-quality conversations. Deloitte, The Gap, and Adobe have already discarded their evaluation forms and freed "human capital" from various further unnecessary formalities. At Red Bull, corresponding local initiatives have always been replaced by a global feedback and performance coaching system.

Red Bull did not need a Human Resources department during the first fifteen years. From 2004, with the company's growth and international expansion, also in the Anglo-American countries, it became necessary to organize the personnel work from Fuschl am See. This personnel work is directed largely by the convictions of the founder Dietrich Mateschitz and the doctrines of Viktor Frankl. From the beginning, all staff measures at Red Bull were required to pass the Frankl Test. If they guarantee a sensible amount of room for maneuver, they will encourage personal responsibility and self-transcendence, they will place a focus on talent, strengths, and meaning, and will strengthen confidence in oneself and in each other. Frankl and Mateschitz encourage us to act freely and independently, so that we will devote ourselves to a task—if necessary, unconditionally—and will remain confident and optimistic, even under adverse conditions. If a measure does not comply with these principles, it will not be implemented. And because many of the usual human resources instruments predominantly serve control and central regulation, it is not surprising that they fail to pass the Frankl Test at Red Bull.

THOUGHTS ON THE FUTURE OF WORK – AN EPILOGUE

" Human behavior will not be dictated by conditions which people encounter, but by decisions which they take themselves. "

VIKTOR FRANKL

A world in turmoil

Over long periods, the history of the world of work has been one of the dominance of a small number of players over numerous chess pieces. Following industrialization, the trades governed by the guilds, in which the work was still closely linked with the master craftsmen, died out. From that point onward, work processes were defined in minute detail and compartmentalized, with the aim of completing the task as efficiently as possible. (See the work of Frederick W. Taylor, 1856–1915). Many people today see this as the epitome of the dehumanization of work. Work processes are defined in minute detail and compartmentalized, with the aim of completing the task as efficiently as possible, with humans as a factor that can be replaced at any time. Process control and time tracking ensure that the system functions without a hitch. The result is routine work, remote-controlled and uninteresting, with the individual as "nothing but" a production factor, and hence the embodiment of the reductionism that Viktor Frankl so often criticized. The work is carried out because it is paid for, mostly poorly rather than fairly. Creativity, development, and opportunities for such development are not the most important elements in this environment. Today we live in an information society, in which the humanization and democratization of the world of work are highly developed. In spite of these developments, it is astonishing how our working environment in many sectors continues to cling to anachronistic thought patterns from the industrial society, thereby preventing self-determination and the search for meaning.

In the coming decades, companies will be challenged to a greater degree than ever before in our history. Digitalization will make many occupations obsolete; some estimates assume that half of all jobs could disappear. Many new occupations will be created. The details of how quickly this will happen, and how radically Big Data, the Internet of Things, and Artificial Intelligence (AI) will change our world of work, is the subject of controversy. Yet everyone agrees that jobs requiring few qualifications are very likely to become automated, and therefore that here in particular a large number of employment opportunities will disappear. The new professions, especially in the commercial fields of strategic planning and in e-learning as well as in IT, finance, and human resources, will demand higher qualifications. That will be a challenge for society as a whole, for employees, for companies, and also for the education and social system.

An example from the world of Red Bull: Roland Concin has a science doctorate and was the Operations factotum in the company. He began to equip the filling installations at Rauch with sensors, in order to recognize quality deviations in the production at an early stage, thereby enabling rapid intervention. Concin was not an AI expert, but he implemented it in a practical manner and enabled Red Bull to avoid destroying cans, thereby keeping the consumption of raw materials to a minimum.

The economist Erik Brynjolfsson, former Director of the Institute for Digital Economics at the Massachusetts Institute of Technology (MIT) and author of the book *The Second Machine Age*, speaks in this context from the Winner-Takes-All phenomenon. Creative employees who are able to make use via AI of the chances of the huge data sets arising in virtually all processes will make the crucial difference. Firms that do not take advantage of this potential, on the other hand, will share the fate of the dinosaurs.

Those who best master the upheaval as a society will take over the leading economic role in the world economy in the medium and long term. With its *corporate social credit system*, China is banking on total data supervision and control. In the country with a single political party and collective surveillance, the plus-minus system which already applies to the individual citizen will also be transferred to companies. Data from all areas of a company—there is talk of thirty areas and 300 factors—will have to be supplied to the authorities and will be evaluated by them. Those who have too few points will be heavily taxed, or will not receive any further permits or orders. One can be sure of transparent constitutional and fair application, as always when it is a question of China. America is banking on GAFA, its "Gang of Four" technology giants: Google, Amazon, Facebook, and Apple. "Big Tech" is to ensure that the USA can save its technological advantage by helping it across the finishing line of the imminent transformation. Then, when the contest has been decided, when diesel and electric cars belong to the distant past, and driverless cars with fuel cells *made in the USA* dominate, the companies will be broken up, as happened with Rockefeller and Standard Oil only just over a century ago. America's institutions, robust and equipped with authority, chutzpah, and a sense of their own power, will survive anyway.

And Europe? First of all, Europe must speak with a single voice. Henry Kissinger once remarked that he did not know whom he should call if he wanted to speak to Europe. China is building the new Silk Road, and the United States are driving technological progress forward, while Europe is mainly quarreling amongst itself. In the meantime, Brussels is drawing up norms for the color of signposts on footpaths (according to DIN 33466 yellow, but in line with the Swiss model) and the maximum curvature of cucumbers (until 2009 a top-class salad cucumber was permitted a maximum curvature of one centimeter per ten centimeters of length). Data protection will cripple entire branches of industry without weighing up the difference between the justified interests of consumers and companies and the already excessive trouble caused by complainers. The British, now with obligations only to free trade and the balance of power on the continent, were so disgusted by the bureaucracy and gold plating in the member states that they have already left the single shop and prefer—admittedly seduced and lied to—to sink in the chaos of Brexit. The European Union will only avoid sinking if they succeed in achieving what the Imperial and Royal Monarchy of Austria-Hungary achieved with its multinational state: a joint foreign, financial, and defence policy, preferably in a Europe with far-reaching regional autonomy.

Regardless of who will eventually take over the leading role in this century, in the medium and long term we are heading for a *single* world. Digitalization works here like a fire accelerant or a catalyst, depending on your point of view. Yuval Noah Harari described the advancing globalization in his books. Looking back shows impressively how systematically aggression has been forced back. Culture always leads to the elimination of aggression. We are speaking here of individual aggression, not of war, which as we know is the continuation of politics. By mobilizing the masses, culture leads to war and trade, and hence to an exchange of genes across ethnic groups. And just as currently, after millions of years of selection and intermingling, only *Homo sapiens* has survived, in a not-too-distant future there will be only one race, one type, one culture, and one society. Real-time data make our world fuse together. Just as Stefan Zweig longed for a united Europe in peace, the humanist hopes for a transformation to a peaceful world in future. May we have better luck than the generations before us, and may our children be spared from bashing each other's brains out yet again, because this time—thanks to human genius and progress—the club they will be using will be an atomic one.

Homo oeconomicus and reasonable average man versus the knowledge worker

Man longs for perfection. In the economic sciences it is *Homo oeconomicus*, and in jurisprudence it is the average consumer, who embodies this ideal image. Since the second half of the twentieth century, the economic sciences have been dominated more than any other by the Chicago School of thought around Milton Friedman. As in the Catholic Church in the Middle Ages, top positions in politics, business, and the media are distributed among its representatives. The University of Chicago has produced more than twice as many Nobel prizewinners as Harvard and Princeton together. Their catechism is pure market economy, in which financial capital is unregulated since it can choose between serving the real economy or only itself. We "thank" it for neo-classical price theory, and for the dogma that the free markets are the most efficient means of allocating resources and distributing income. The excesses of this freedom are the nationalization of debts from the last bank bailout, and the associated rise in national debt as well as zombie firms, which can survive only under the conditions of a zero-interest policy. Under the opinion leadership of neoliberalism, the room for maneuver for politics is reduced to virtually zero.

In the neo-classical model, people decide purely rationally according to a mechanistic cost-benefit model. Underlying this model is the "invisible hand," which supposedly leads to absolute market transparency. This theorem of the rational agent, who for decades has wandered as *Homo oeconomicus* through game theory and the economic sciences, exclusively maximizing use and largely unreflectingly, has only one small fault: it does not correspond to reality. The mathematical equilibrium models of the Chicago School disregard the ability to learn and the freedom of decision of the individual, his "marginal actions" wherever there is change—indeed, the actions of real people. They fail to see that each individual person has the freedom to make his or her own free choices ... and they do. Here, they contrast with the Austrian School around Carl Menger and Ludwig von Mises, which does not reduce people to mere objects influenced by material factors.

What *Homo oeconomicus* represents for the economic sciences, that is the average consumer (*reasonable average man*) for the legal sector. He, too, is a constructed creature, perfect in theory (averagely well informed, attentive, and sensible), and in practice, "a botched job." And he too is condemned to fail when faced with reality. Wherever we encounter the reasonable average man, universally valued by judges and severely overworked, we can expect no mercy.

However, we not only long for perfection in ourselves, but we also wish, if not for a perfect world, then at least for a perfect organization. But like everything made by human hand, organizations are not perfect either, and we have to decide: Do we want an effective or a perfect company? Organizations that strive for perfection tend to "over engineer," to constant re-organization and regrouping, process optimization, and the marginalization of the human factor. The potential factor of human work proves itself to be too uncertain in the parade of the other production factors which are all calculable. Wherever the demands are optimized as far as possible and raised, the environment and the company are inhuman, and a feeling of powerlessness and loss of control arises; timetables and deadlines can no longer be kept. And that in turn leads to the staff being seen as "nothing but" a cost factor to be controlled as far as possible.

In our striving for superhuman perfection, the specifically human aspect and the value of humankind as a human resource is lost: the individual as a knowledge worker. Everything that reduces the individual and his or her uniqueness is bound to cause frustration. Only if we accept that people are inevitably superior to systems and technologies, can we do justice to humankind as a human resource. Only people have unusual ideas, surprising insights, and manifold experiences, and are capable through their combined knowledge of judging and not just measuring. People as knowledge workers invent new products and services. Only they can rush on ahead of their time, anticipate future developments and technologies, and hence bring about progress. Only the interplay of many knowledge workers will allow companies to achieve top performances. Humans with their visionary thinking provide the foundations on which organizations can think up new things. Therefore people must be at the heart of each organization. Companies are there for people and not vice-versa; they are the catalyst for innovation which can only be produced by people. Let us not forget that all systems, processes, and statistics always serve only to effect quantitative measurement and never contribute to the inventive spirit that is necessary in order to produce creative work from which we and others can benefit.

Humans as a success factor

A business community in which people and their success form the hub is in any case preferable to thinking exclusively in terms of shareholder value. As we know, for Dietrich Mateschitz the maximizing of profits was not an incentive. He even believed that in exceptional cases one also had a right to make an irrational decision, especially when it was a matter of honor. Such a freedom of conscience and decision-making is healthy for the corporate culture, but is only possible if one is not under an obligation to anonymous shareholders. It is only decisions like these that make a corporate culture based on decency possible.

Much has been written about the nuisance and the excesses of the shareholder-value approach. It is one of the fringe areas of an economics in which business finance leads a life of its own and no longer serves the real economy. The quarterly reports which with their key profit figures are so important for financial capital on the stock exchanges, determine business activity. Companies run by their owners find it easier to invest in market shares, innovation, and knowledge workers, and if necessary to set other priorities. Investments in Latin America are a good example of this. The currency fluctuations, taxes, and political developments make business planning difficult. At around the turn of the millennium, McKinsey estimated the Brazilian market for energy drinks in the long term as not more than one hundred million cans. Today the market is a multiple larger thereof, and growth continues. Nonetheless, the macroeconomic framework conditions are not easy, and profit forecasts are regularly nullified by new tax laws and currency fluctuations. The euro is sometimes worth two real, and then again worth four real. Instead of reacting to such catastrophes with austerity programs and cost cutting across all areas, Red Bull can afford to invest anticyclically. In stormy times we shall be satisfied with breaking even and thereby strengthen our market shares, and in good times, the profits will be even better. While traditional companies are forced to manage their cash flow and profits in line with the expectations of pension funds and funds managers at BlackRock, Red Bull is free to do what is right for the company and its long-term growth: to invest in people and ideas.

"All organizations say as a matter of routine that people are their greatest capital asset. But very few actually practice what they preach, let alone really believe in it," says Peter Drucker. As a humanist he is interested first of all in people and only then in companies. Even in our service society, he still sees the decisive success factor in companies, with their technologization, automation, and Big Data, as people, whose unique abilities are irreplaceable. Top performance depends more than ever on the new knowledge workers in companies. Knowledge workers whom we choose to the best of our knowledge and ability on the basis of their willingness and ability to perform, and who we confidently encourage to act freely and responsibly, so that they can find the right tasks and make a meaningful contribution to the aims of the company—ideally oblivious to self and with equanimity.

Whichever economic sphere we consider, the progress of globalization will compel companies to respond to the expectations and wishes of the new knowledge workers. Even more than today, in the second age of the machine, this new generation will form the backbone of the economy that has been transformed by digitalization. Companies which see their employees as a cost factor and not as creative potential, will look like old fools, but will not live that long. These employees want more than merely to earn money. They value a professional environment in which talent encounters talent in order to create more knowledge, and in which a career depends on completing tasks and not on politics. The knowledge workers of tomorrow long for professional challenges in a digital world, not for collective wages and limited working hours. Work will be global but life will be regional, and national states inclined towards paternalism and client politics will crumble.

With serenity to new ideas

The neurobiologist Gerald Hüther, Head of the Department of Neurological Foundational Research at the Psychiatric Clinic of the University of Göttingen, points out that "Inner serenity and letting go ... [can] trigger creative processes in our brain. In order to have a really new idea, to be creative, you must not just focus on one particular thing; you must be in a state in which you have activated countless networks in the brain at the same time, and only then, when you have activated countless areas in the brain simultaneously, can this miracle take place which occurs sometimes, that you can link together things which you would not normally combine in the stress of everyday life, and then new ideas and new thoughts arise, so to speak."*

Children especially need serenity and leisure above all, in order to arrive at new ideas and to invent things. Instead of which, they are frequently subjected to constant sensory overload and the hustle and bustle of the adult world. "It is possible that, in the stress of the modern age in which we live, we have already transferred our ideas too much to our children and believe that if we rush around so hectically that they too will have to learn it soon enough," writes Hüther. "You can do that, but unfortunately it then leads to the fact that the children will have difficulty realizing this wonderful diverse potential that they are born with ... In a time and in a society where everyone races round like mad, we can say that they all function quite well and perhaps they all also fulfill their tasks quite well, but they are

---

* For this and the following quotation, see Gerald Hüther, *Was wir sind und was wir sein könnten: Ein neurobiologischer Mutmacher*, Frankfurt am Main, 2013.

all unlikely to develop the creative potential that they would need in order to really develop further, to create new ideas. And so, in this hectic society, we are gradually losing the spirit of innovation. That is something that nowadays many companies complain about, which attempted in the past to increase the pressure in order to become more and more effective. But this focus on efficiency is at the cost of the spirit of innovation within the company."

Dietrich Mateschitz agreed with this analysis without reservation. Being able to switch off and remain calm is a requirement for creativity and new ideas. He repeatedly asked what all our employees were doing every day that was so important while they were sitting in front of their computers. When did they have time to think about new ideas?

The top-class performance of knowledge workers cannot be called up digitally by simply pressing a button. It arises in a space that is characterized by meaning, serenity, and the release of "human potential." In 1967, long before digitalization and at the beginning of the service society, Peter Drucker wrote in his classic work *The Effective Executive*: "The unique purpose of an organization is to make strengths productive. Of course, it cannot overcome the weaknesses which each and every one of us possesses in abundance. But it can make them irrelevant." Meaning, talent, and strengths have not formed the focus of effective management since the founding of Positive Psychology. What many people do not know or perhaps do not want to know so precisely, is that with these principles they are following derive from the central thoughts of Viktor Frankl.

On true freedom

We started this book with a chapter on freedom and personal responsibility. And now it will close with a summary of the poem of the Grand Inquisitor in Dostoevsky's *The Brothers Karamazov*, and with a few concluding thoughts on freedom.

During the sixteenth century, during an autodafé in Seville, "at a stroke almost one hundred heretics" were burned at the stake to the great glory of God. Jesus Christ appeared again on Earth "still and inconspicuously" on the next day for the first time after fifteen hundred years, "and lo, something strange happened. Everyone recognized him." The people followed him. He made a blind man see again, and awakened a girl from the dead to life. Thereupon a high priest had him arrested and thrown into prison.

In the "dark, hot, motionless" night, the priest visited Jesus in the dungeon. "Are you he?"—"Yes!", he said. He must leave the Church in peace. He had nothing to add to his work; he would only cause disruption and produce further confusion. After all, he had "transferred everything to the Pope."

The people called for bread, miracles, and submission. They did not want the freedom for which he had sacrificed himself, but preferred to live as slaves and under tutelage. People fear nothing more than the freedom into which they were born, and there is nothing they would rather do than pass on the "gift of freedom" to the next-best person. For this reason, the Church would strive to acquire all power and would distribute the bread it had previously taken away from the people. And it would bring about holy miracles in the secret of faith. At that time, when the "spirit of self annihilation and non-being" visited him in the wilderness,

Jesus should have succumbed to the temptation to take over the power; now the Church had to fulfill this mission. "In accepting the kingdom of the world and Caesar's purple, one would find a universal kingdom and secure to mankind eternal peace. And who can rule mankind better than those who have possessed themselves of man's conscience, and hold in their hand man's daily bread? Having accepted Caesar's glaive and purple, we had, of course, but to deny Thee, to henceforth follow him alone. Oh, centuries of intellectual riot and rebellious free thought are yet before us, and their science will end by anthropophagy." For eight hundred years they had been serving the devil, and there was still no end in sight.

Jesus spoke not a single word and kissed the ninety-five-year-old priest on the mouth, whereupon the latter no longer had him burned at the stake on the next day, as announced, but sent him "out into the dark streets and squares of the city." Not without warning him not to return.

The three temptations—to change stones into bread, to throw himself down from the temple and be caught by the angels of the Lord, and to rule over all the kingdoms of this world—are those offered to him by Satan in St. Matthew's gospel, chapter 4, v. 1–10. They are the great questions of humanity, which all the wise men in the world would not have been "able to think up, but from an ... eternal absolute ... Because in these questions lies as it were the entire future history of the human race, summarized and prophesied."

Nothing is more detrimental to freedom than the temptations of Satan: immoderateness, superstition, and abuse of power. Everywhere where the alert spirit capitulates before the invasion of bread and wine, body and blood, the profane decadence of excesses, the comedies and power games, and the Machiavellianism will rule. The same applies to deeply felt half-truths of belief and superstition in supposedly mystic-cryptic transubstantiation. What good fortune is that in which freedom is overwhelmed and laid at the feet of a power, and the people say: "Enslave us if you prefer, but give us enough to eat." Bread was despised for the sake of freedom. For Dostoevsky, the true believer does not lay his freedom at the feet of any authority. He does not allow himself to be tranquilized and patronized by "Miracle, Mystery, and Authority."

"For the secret of human existence does not exist in simply living, but in what one lives for. If one has no firm idea of the purpose for which one lives, one will no longer wish to continue to live and will rather destroy oneself than remain on Earth—no matter how many loaves of bread lie around one." And whether he has not forgotten "that people find peace and even death preferable to the free will in the knowledge of good and evil? Nothing is more seductive for them than the freedom of conscience, but also nothing is more agonizing." "To decide with a free heart what is good and evil ... instead of following the old laws which have been determined," can we burden man with "a terrible burden, like the freedom of choice?", asks the Grand Inquisitor.

For the Church, man is "weak and vicious." Its secret is that it is not his ally, but that of the Devil and that "at last all will unite together and unanimously in a comprehensive antheap which no one will dispute." Since the majority of humankind cannot come to terms with freedom, and for them "it does not mean a great moral happiness to achieve the perfection of the will," it is necessary to "make use of lies and deception, to consciously lead people to death and destruction and in doing so to deceive them the whole time... so that they do not notice where they are being led, so that these poor blind souls at least believe on their journey that they are happy."

Nothing could characterize the endeavors and legacy of Dietrich Mateschitz better than Dostoevsky's tale of the Grand Inquisitor. The lessons also sketch out the great questions of the Enlightenment and anticipate the way of thinking of Viktor Frankl. Wherever individual freedom is suppressed by predominantly institutional temptations and reprisals, freedom must be defended with increased reasoning power, vigilance, alertness, and watchfulness. Only in the reef of the watchful spirit which faces the uncertain, which prefers to eat its own bread, which refuses to sing the songs of others, will we come—whether rich or poor—into the heaven of devotion.

The long line of Enlightenment philosophers warns us to make use of our intellect without instructions from others. To be bold and follow our conscience in distinguishing between Good and Evil. For freedom we shall have to pass Kafka's doorkeeper and, like him, question the superstition and faith of a "chosen people" as well as our own. To break out from the mass of "geese," to be neither a deceived member of the flock nor a deceiving shepherd, but to become a giant and to complete the construction of the Tower of Babel. If we succeed in that, we shall discover, as it were, as the supreme event, that despite external dependencies, we have ultimately found inner freedom.

Dostoevsky and Frankl were deeply religious, while Mateschitz and Kafka were atheists. This is only an apparent contradiction, for according to Dostoevsky the true atheist is only one small step away from the believer. Both, the true believer and the doubting atheist, are nonetheless united in the absolute belief in the freedom of will and the will to find freedom and meaning.

ACKNOWLEDGMENTS

This book could not have been published without the enthusiastic support of a number of people. I should like to thank them all.

First and foremost, I would like to thank Dietrich Mateschitz posthumously, who, without ever intending to, has been a fatherly advisor to me and made this book possible in every respect.

And then especially Mark Mateschitz. Not only for reading it and enriching it with some additional anecdotes, but also for granting his permission to publish *Dietrich Mateschitz: Wings for People and Ideas* after his father's death.

I should also like to thank Stefan Salzer. He, too, took the time to read the text, especially the passages on HR topics, and in particular with regard to some of the statistics he was more accurate than I was.

I am also grateful to Claudia Hubbauer for her valuable support with many aspects of the project. I greatly appreciate her wise tips and assessments regarding numerous passages in the text.

Thanks to Peter White for his invaluable comments and input on the English version of this book.

And then my thanks are also due to the team at Benevento Publishing, the publishing company of Red Bull Media House: Christoph Loidl for his project management, which has been characterized by good-natured calmness in the best Franconian manner; Stefan Mayr for his understanding of the text and remarkable conceptual work; and Caroline Metzger for her professional and careful copy-editing.

FURTHER READING BY VIKTOR FRANKL

Ärztliche Seelsorge, 7th edition. Munich: DTV, 2017.
Bergerlebnis und Sinnerfahrung, with photos by Christian Handl. Innsbruck: Tyrolia, 2013.
Das Leiden am sinnlosen Leben: Psychotherapie für heute. Freiburg: Herder, 2015.
Der leidende Mensch: Anthropologische Grundlagen der Psychotherapie, 3rd edition. Bern: Huber, 2005.
Der Mensch vor der Frage nach dem Sinn: Eine Auswahl aus dem Gesamtwerk. Munich: Piper, 1996.
Der unbewusste Gott: Psychotherapie und Religion, 14th edition. Munich: DTV, 2017.
Der Wille zum Sinn: Ausgewählte Vorträge über Logotherapie, 7th edition. Bern: Hogrefe, 2016 (Engl.: *The Will to Meaning: Foundations and Applications of Logotherapy*. New York: Plume, 1988).
Die eine Menschheit: Appelle für den Frieden, with a foreword by Wolfgang Schüssel. Salzburg/Munich: Benevento, 2023.
Die Sinnfrage in der Psychotherapie, 6th edition. Munich: Piper, 1996.
Logotherapie und Existenzanalyse, 3rd edition. Weinheim/Basel: Beltz, 2010.
Man's Search for Meaning: An Introduction to Logotherapy, London: Ebury, 2004.
Man's Search for Ultimate Meaning: A revised and extended edition of The Unconscious God, with a foreword by Swanee Hunt. New York: Insight Books, 1997.

Psychotherapy and Existentialism: Selected Papers on Logotherapy. New York: Washington Square Press, 1967.

Theorie und Therapie der Neurosen: Einführung in Logotherapie und Existenzanalyse, 9th edition. Munich: UTB, 2007 (Engl.: *On the Theory and Therapy of Mental Disorders: An Introduction to Logotherapy and Existential Analysis,* translated by James M. DuBois. New York: Routledge, 2004).

Über den Sinn des Lebens: Mit einem Vorwort von Joachim Bauer, 3rd edition. Weinheim/Basel: Beltz, 2020.

Was nicht in meinen Büchern steht: Lebenserinnerungen, Weinheim/Basel: Beltz, 2002 (Engl.: *Recollections: An Autobiography,* London: Basic, 2000).

Zeiten der Besinnung: Gleichnisse, with a foreword by Walter Kohl, compiled and expanded, and with a commentary by Elisabeth Lukas. Salzburg/Munich: Benevento, 2023.

Zeiten der Entscheidung: *Ermutigungen,* with a foreword by Alexander Batthyány, compiled and updated, and with a commentary and an afterword by Elisabeth Lukas, Salzburg/Munich: Benevento, 2022.

Volker Viechtbauer was a close companion of Dietrich Mateschitz for many years. He is not only familiar with his career as an entrepreneur, but also with his fascination for the thinking and ideas of Viktor Frankl. Viechtbauer himself is an avid reader of literature and non-fiction. He lives with his family near Salzburg.